Characteristics of the Successful Twenty-First Century Information Professional

CHANDOS
INFORMATION PROFESSIONAL SERIES

Series Editor: Ruth Rikowski
(email: rikowskigr@aol.com)

Chandos' new series of books are aimed at the busy information professional. They have been specially commissioned to provide the reader with an authoritative view of current thinking. They are designed to provide easy-to-read and (most importantly) practical coverage of topics that are of interest to librarians and other information professionals. If you would like a full listing of current and forthcoming titles, please visit our web site **www.chandospublishing.com** or contact Hannah Grace-Williams on email info@chandospublishing.com or telephone number +44 (0) 1865 884447.

New authors: we are always pleased to receive ideas for new titles; if you would like to write a book for Chandos, please contact Dr Glyn Jones on email gjones@chandospublishing.com or telephone number +44 (0) 1865 884447.

Bulk orders: some organisations buy a number of copies of our books. If you are interested in doing this, we would be pleased to discuss a discount. Please contact Hannah Grace-Williams on email info@chandospublishing.com or telephone number +44 (0) 1865 884447.

Characteristics of the Successful Twenty-First Century Information Professional

DENNIE HEYE

Chandos Publishing

Oxford · England

Chandos Publishing (Oxford) Limited
Chandos House
5 & 6 Steadys Lane
Stanton Harcourt
Oxford OX29 5RL
UK
Tel: +44 (0) 1865 884447 Fax: +44 (0) 1865 884448
Email: info@chandospublishing.com
www.chandospublishing.com

First published in Great Britain in 2006

ISBN:
1 84334 145 X (paperback)
1 84334 197 2 (hardback)

© D. Heye, 2006

Typeset by Domex e-Data Pvt. Ltd.
Printed in the UK and USA.

Contents

Preface

Writing a book has always been a dream of mine, especially about the key elements of my profession. So I was excited to be approached by Glyn Jones of Chandos Publishing to actually write one. It took nine months, many hours behind my computer, endless series of cups of tea, a dozen new grey hairs and lots of classic rock music to finally come to what you are now holding in your hands.

This book would not have been possible without the support of my wonderful wife Eveline, who always supported me during the whole process and gently persuaded me to write when I didn't feel like writing...

Also thanks to all those inspiring colleagues, managers and peers I have met over the years who all helped me to improve myself continuously as an information professional.

About the author

Dennie Heye is an information scientist at the library of a Fortune 500 global energy firm, responsible for library innovation, electronic content acquisition and information architecture projects. He has been a key member of global information management projects for his company, providing expert input on information architecture.

Dennie received his MLS degree in 1993 from the Bibliotheek & Documentaire Informatie School in Maastricht, with a final thesis focusing on the role of new media in the curriculum of Dutch library schools.

In 1996 he acquired a Master of Arts degree on information science marketing and sociology from the University in Tilburg. His final thesis was on the set-up of a commercial telephone enquiry service for small and medium-sized businesses.

From 1996 to 2002 he worked as knowledge manager and literature searcher in the Deloitte & Touche Information Resource Center in Amsterdam. Here he played a vital role in the conversion of the library and archive to a state-of-the-art hybrid information centre. In 1997 he was on the pioneering team for the first Deloitte & Touche intranet in the Netherlands, responsible for information architecture. From 2000 to 2002 he played a leading role in the set-up and implementation of the document management system for his department, writing the cookbook for further implementation on tagging, folder structures and document policy guidelines.

Dennie has spoken and published about library and information science issues, mainly on innovative solutions and services marketing. His main interests are taxonomies, library 2.0 and information architecture. That said, he is still able to dress himself and carry out simple tasks.

The author may be contacted via the following:

E-mail: *dennie@heye.nl*
Website: *http://www.dennie.heye.nl*

Introduction

First of all, thank you for showing an interest in my book! The best compliment an author can get is being read and enhancing the reader's life – in this case helping you to become a more successful information professional.

In my view, being an information professional today is one of the most exciting professions: helping others to organise, navigate and manage information in this increasingly information-centric world. With our skill set and a continuous evolution of technology, we can play a key role in companies, organisations and society.

Being an information professional, however, requires certain characteristics to transform successfully into a twenty-first century information professional, constantly reinventing themselves to stay relevant. As technology, user behaviour and information needs constantly change, we have to adopt – meaning we must also constantly change. This change does not threaten our profession, but is an excellent driver to become key players and linking pins in the information ecology.

Based on my ten years of experience as an information professional, I have tried to capture the most important characteristics of the successful twenty-first century information professional to solve the most job-critical challenges. Most of the topics in this book have been addressed in other books, but not from the viewpoint of an information professional, in one practical volume.

This book aims to be practical and insightful, and I hope it will be helpful to all my peers who want to constantly learn, evolve and be the best information professional they can be. The book is structured to describe the 16 most essential characteristics I have identified from my own experience and studies like the SLA 'Competencies for Information Professionals'. The characteristics range from core information professional skills like information searching and information architecture, to broader skills like presentation skills and project management. I have tried to capture the essence of each characteristic in one chapter with practical tips and ideas how to increase your own level of the specific characteristic. The book can be read from cover to cover, or by selectively reading the relevant chapters for your specific interests.

The book should give you practical advice and insights in how to become a successful information professional with all the characteristics needed to play that vital role in your organisation. All the ideas and tips in the book have been described in a concise format, so you can apply them quickly.

I appreciate your feedback to this book at any time, as I too still learn every day and mostly from others. Find out more about me, and, by all means, please contact me via the website or e-mail mentioned in the 'About the author' section.

You are creative and keen to innovate

This chapter captures two important and closely linked 'soft skill' topics for information professionals:

- *Creativity*: In general, this is the production of new ideas or combining old ideas in a new way; it is also the main driver for innovation.
- *Innovation*: This is the transformation of a new idea into a new product or service, or an improvement in organisation or process

Creativity and innovation are a bit magical: it is very hard to be creative on the spot, but by creating the right atmosphere and keeping an open mind, the magic can appear. As Tom Kelly, author of *The Art of Innovation*, once said: 'the spark of innovation is not in *what* we do, but in *how* we do it'.

Information professionals and innovation

First, I would like to discuss what innovation and creativity can do for us as information professionals, and then I will present tips and techniques to stimulate creativity and innovative thinking.

As information professionals, we live in exciting times. With information management now more important than ever, new tools and creative ideas to help people manage information are being introduced almost weekly. Consider the developments in information retrieval in the last ten years: Internet search engines, wikis, peer-to-peer file sharing, blogs and so on.

As an example, take a look at the development of Internet search engines over the past ten years. In 1996 the Internet was starting to catch on as the new information platform, and we saw the start of full-text search engines like Yahoo! Looking back, the capabilities of those early search engines were limited: they had an index of only one or two million web pages, could only index HTML and text files, and ranking was based on word frequency. In 1996, however, this was a major tool for information retrieval: for the world at large, this was unprecedented access to a wide range of information using a search engine that was simple to use. Now, in 2006, search engines add features every few months and become more versatile: billions of web pages indexed, all common document formats can be indexed, more intelligent ranking, with categorisation on the fly (e.g. Vivisimo). The launch of Google Earth has shown us yet another innovative look at information, and this is just the tip of the iceberg of innovative information management tools.

This illustrates that the innovation rate in information management is high, and that innovation and creativity can lead to new and exciting tools and services. In addition, it is not just about us creating new tools and services, as information professionals we can also help our organisations in supporting innovation:

- *Disseminate information*: We can find internal and external information relevant to innovation for our organisations. We should not just send information as we find it, but extract the main messages related to our organisation (i.e. put it into context) and deliver this to key groups involved in the innovation process.

- *Provide resources*: Such as books, journals and electronic resources related to innovation and creativity.

- *Act as a linking pin*: As information professionals, we have networks inside and outside our organisations. We can recognise opportunities for innovation and pass them on to the right people, if possible supported by documentation (e.g. a patent search or links to press clippings).

Creativity and innovation tips

Even if you would not describe yourself as very creative, you can develop your creative skills or facilitate sessions where creativity is needed.

Take a risk

There is no innovation without risk. You will propose something different and new, which has not been proven or accepted. So there is a risk your idea will not work, be criticised, not supported or even fail. But if you do not dare to risk all of this, your innovation will just remain an idea. Recognise the type of risk involved with your idea, for example, whether financial or ethical; whether it will it be accepted in the culture you work in; or whether your organisation, your customer or the world is ready for your innovation. When you have a good feeling what the risk of your innovation entails, you can estimate the chances of that risk happening. In the end it comes down to the question whether the risk outweighs the opportunity of your innovation.

I wish...

When you were a kid, you used to close your eyes weeks before Christmas or your birthday and wish for the best present you could imagine. In your mind you could see, almost touch that awesome present you wanted most of all.

As an adult, you can use the same wishing process to start a creative concept. Start with a wish that would help you in your life or work. This could be 'I wish I could finish this large project on time, but still have time to enjoy my gourmet cooking class'. This wish can then be translated into a deeper wish, which in this case could be 'I wish I could learn how to prioritise in my life and maintain a good work–life balance'.

This can then lead into a creative thought process how to achieve this much desired goal.

Visualising

Related to the wishing concept is visualisation. Try to visualise in your mind what your want to achieve, for example, a redesign of your library. Think of all the details how that redesigned library would look. What colour is the floor? What feeling do you get in the new library? Where is the front desk located? How do you walk from the entrance to the reading table? By building a very clear picture in your head, your motivation to achieve this will increase and you will also know exactly what you want and how you want it to be.

Daydream

Do you remember how your mind just freezes when you want it to come up with an original idea or a solution for a problem on the spot? And how it just pops into your mind when you are staring out the window or relaxing by listening to some music?

I usually get my best ideas when I cleaning the bathroom. For some strange reason, by doing something as mundane as rinsing the tiles and mopping the floor, my mind relaxes and my subconsciousness kicks in with great ideas.

Turn it upside down

You may find yourself stuck thinking about a certain problem and unable to find inspiration. A useful trick in situations like this is to turn your problem upside down. For instance, you want to find new ways how to attract new users to your online portal. Now, turn the problem upside down: how could you make the situation worse, i.e. how could you drive users away from your online portal?

In this case, you could use a terrible user interface, with a typeface that is hard to read. Never update the portal. Put all relevant information at least three clicks away. Completely ignore all the feedback from users. And last, but not least, implement a search engine that never finds relevant information.

You will be surprised, especially if you do this in a team setting, how quickly you will get a list of 'how to make this worse' items. After a certain time, or when you have gathered a good list of items, you can use this list to find out what you should be doing.

Be curious

In order to become and stay creative, you need to encourage your brain to embrace creativity. You can do this by regularly learning about new things, which keeps your mind fresh and makes it easier to relate between different topics. So make it a habit to study something new every once in a while, be it a new language, a new hobby or a topic that just seems interesting. What can you learn about it? How does this new topic relate to what you already now?

SWOT analysis

A SWOT analysis is a strategic planning tool used to evaluate the strengths, weaknesses, opportunities, and threats related a new project or organisation. A SWOT analysis is often done in a brainstorm type setting with a team of different people related to the new project or organisation, where openness and creativity are key ingredients.

Strengths and weaknesses come from inside the organisation, and opportunities and threats originate from outside:

■ a strength might be what you do well – aspects where you add value, key processes, a special expertise;

■ a weakness is what could be improved, non-value added aspects, poor image or lack of expertise in an area;

■ an opportunity can be a trend in the market, strategic alliances, new developing markets or a competitor underperforming;

■ threats are obstacles you are being faced with, such as stricter government legislation related to your product or service, competitors with better technology or price wars in the market where you are operating.

By working with a group of people who have different perspectives on the project or organisation, you will create a 'picture' that provides direction and serves as a basis for the development of marketing plans.

With the SWOT analysis at hand, try to find:

- the opportunities that match with the strengths;

- the weaknesses that can be overcome by the opportunities;

- the strengths that can help you cope with the threats;

- the weaknesses that should be analysed to make them less susceptible to the threats.

Post-It power brainstorm

I am always very fond of this technique, where a focus team uses the 'power' of Post-It notes to tackle problems or create new ideas. Split the audience into smaller groups, each no fewer than three but no more than seven members. Each team is given a problem or a topic to discuss, for example, how to create a successful induction strategy for new recruits.

Each team member gets a stack of Post-It notes and has ten minutes to write down as many ideas, solutions, brainwaves, clues and aspects as possible. After ten minutes, the team leader asks each member to stick all the notes to a whiteboard. Once this is done, the team reviews the notes and groups together related themes, for example, all ideas related to IT tools or human resources etc.

Duplicates can be created to indicate that this idea or solution is considered to be more relevant to the group. Through this activity, certain patterns and relationships can be generated, providing a good basis to solve a problem or develop a new strategy.

Learn from your mistakes

When you do something new or different, there is always a chance of making a mistake. The creative idea you had to solve a conflict between two teams by inviting them to an off-site bakery where they had to bake cakes together may have resulted in a lot of dough on the floor, angry words and you feeling bad.

Don't let this scare you away from new and creative paths, but learn from it. Mistakes show you what did not work and should be analysed so you can do better next time. If Michelangelo had thrown away his paint brushes after his first concept sketches of the ceiling of the Sistine Chapel, we would never have seen this miraculous painting.

Meet with different people

To a certain extent, your ideas are influenced by the people with whom you interact. Most likely, you will work with the same people for quite some time – which can create tunnel vision in your thinking. By meeting different people you will hear new perspectives, be challenged on assumptions and be generally more receptive to new ideas. Try and have lunch with a different team once in a while, strike up a conversation while you are queuing or join a new club.

Superheroes

This exercise is very good for developing a creative atmosphere in a group, so a subsequent activity (e.g. a SWOT analysis) will benefit from the level of openness and creativity.

Group members are confronted by a problem and have to solve it by pretending to be a superhero like Batman, Superman, Catwoman or even Conan the Librarian. As each superhero has their own special characteristics, people will be triggered to think 'outside the box' and feel less restricted to come up with daring ideas.

New ideas for simple objects

Another exercise to build a creative atmosphere is to let group members think of as many creative uses for simple objects in one minute. For example, what uses for a paperclip or an eraser can they come up with? Give points for the most outrageous ideas and encourage others to build on other members' ideas.

Fresh view

This technique uses the ability of so-called outsiders to provide a fresh view on existing problems. State your problem in a clear way without using jargon, so an outsider will be able to understand it. Invite a few outsiders who have no experience in your field of work to think about the problem. Let them think about it for a few days and write down their thoughts and possible solutions.

When you discuss their ideas, try to leverage them for creative problem-solving even if some ideas seem naive to you. An outsider may have a completely different interpretation of what the real problem is, giving you a new view on the problem and possible solutions.

Reward the outsiders' input by making them understand how valuable their input is and what you did with their ideas. This will make them feel valued and open to help you another time.

3

You are a search engine guru

When the Internet took off in the last decade, we were confronted with a new form of information retrieval tools: search engines. Nowadays, search engines are overtaking the classic, more structured information retrieval methods like databases to help users find information. In order to become an Internet search engine expert, it is important to understand how search engines work so you will be able to use them most effectively.

In this chapter you will learn what different types of search engines exist, how they differ and tips how to increase your success rate in searching.

Directories vs crawler-based search engines

Search engines come in two main varieties: the so-called crawler-based search engines and directories. Table 3.1 summarises the main differences.

Directories

One of the earliest Internet search engines was Yahoo!, which began as a directory search engine, using a subject hierarchy for the web to index websites using human

Table 3.1 The differences between search engines and directories

Directories	Crawler-based search engines
Hand selected sites	All pages in all sites
Search over the contents of the descriptions of the pages	Search over the contents of the pages themselves of the pages
Organised in advance into categories	Organised in response to a query by relevance rankings or other scores
Set up and maintained by human editors	Set up and maintained by computers

Source: Chakrabarti (2002)

editors. For each topic in a directory, an editor selects the most relevant website and adds a description. The websites for each topic are submitted by users or the editors themselves, but it is the editor who decides whether a website is listed in the directory.

So, when you use a directory-based search engine, you are searching an equivalent of the library catalogue: a selected, quality controlled and manually created index of a corpus of information.

The main advantage of a directory search engine is the quality of results, but the disadvantage is the size. As a directory depends on human editors, it cannot cover the same amount of websites as an automated (crawler-based) search engine. Well-known directory based search engines are Yahoo! *(www.yahoo.com)* and The Open Directory *(www.dmoz.org,* which can also be found under the directory tab at Google: *http://www.google.com/dirhp).*

Crawler-based search engines

Crawler-based search engines rely on software, containing advanced algorithms and much computer power to index websites. This type of search engine consists of three different parts:

- crawlers, sometimes called *robots* or *spiders*;
- the indexer;
- the search engine.

The crawler visits a website and starts to read the pages within the website. As each website consists of linked pages, the crawler follows each link on the site to read every page. A copy of all the text on the web page is stored for the indexer, and the crawler looks for links to new web pages. These are then stored in a queue, waiting to be processed. When a page has been processed, the crawler will record the date and time of processing, and start on the next web page in the queue.

As web pages tend to be dynamic, crawlers have an algorithm to find out when a web page needs to be checked for changes. Often this is manually fine-tuned by search engine companies, so websites that are highly dynamic, such as news websites, are crawled daily and more static web pages are checked for changes every three months. It sometimes can take a while for new web pages or changes found by the crawler to be added to the index due to the enormous size of the Web.

The second part is the indexer, which starts with a copy of all the text on the web pages via the crawler. Before the indexer starts, pre-processing is done, and, for example, stop words are removed (e.g. the, and, or), web pages of banned sites are removed and the language of the page is detected. Language detection can later be used to specify one or more languages for the user to limit their search to.

The indexer records all the words, their position, the title of the page, links to other pages, etc. It then creates a reverse index: a long list of all the words in all the web pages, and for each word the index has a pointer to the documents where that particular word occurs.

People use keywords in their searches, so it is far quicker to check if the search engine simply has lists of in which documents particular words occur. Instead of scanning each document for the keywords, the search engine just opens the reverse index list and reports which documents include the words. So, when a user enters a query into the search engine via the Web, the search engine looks through all the pages in its database to find matches to this query. From the matches, a results list is created and then ranked in order of relevancy.

As most users only look at the first ten entries of the results screen, it is key for a search engine to use a good ranking algorithm. How these algorithms are built is the best-kept secret for a search engine company, but it usually involves several of the following:

- *Based on term frequency*: How often the words from the query appear in the page.

- *Font*: Larger or bold fonts often indicate important topics in the page, so when a word from the query appears in a larger or bold font is it considered more relevant.

- *Proximity*: How close the words from the query appear in the page.

- *Position*: Where the words from the query appear in the page. For example, words in the title are considered more relevant than footnotes.

- *Popularity information*: A page containing words from the query and which is referred to by many other pages is considered to be more relevant.

- *Link analysis information*: If the words on the pages that link to a page also contain words from the query, the originator page is considered more relevant.

The last two methods are derived from the ancient art of bibliographic citations, where one looks at who refers to whom to find the most authoritative sources. When many scientific papers that are considered to be very good point to a particular other paper, that other paper must also be good. The web is built on hyperlinks, so many pages link to one another – this is why this methodology generally works well. The best website on a certain topic will surely have many other relevant and popular pages that link to it.

How to become a search engine guru

Now you understand how search engines work, you realise they are not perfect and have to be used correctly. Below are pointers how to increase your search engine expertise.

Considerations regarding search engines

The first consideration to remember is that Internet search engines are not always the best source to use or start with. If you are looking for information that you know you have to pay for, you will not find it for free via a search engine. In addition, as the Web also is a fairly 'young' medium, information from before 1990 can often be very hard.

Second, if you are looking for information on a topic you are not familiar with, it is often faster and more reliable to phone or e-mail someone who is more familiar on the topic. Often that person can point you to a website, journal, book or an expert on that topic before you have developed a good query. In other cases, the same knowledgeable person can help you set up a good query by defining correct keywords and synonyms.

As a third consideration, be aware that the information on the Internet has not been quality checked. When you are using a library catalogue of a journal archive, there is a quality control mechanism on the indexed content. A search engine indexes everything without judgment, which is a pro but surely a con. The principal research rule of validating a source and its content cannot be stressed enough when using a search engine.

Finally, search engines do not cover the entire Internet. Search engines do not index all file formats, and have a size limitation on files indexed. So, for example, only the first megabyte of text from a file will be indexed – and be retrievable. Search engines also have problems indexing dynamic websites, i.e. websites that are created on the fly using database techniques. Instead of linked static pages, dynamic websites create pages from different web components in a database, based on the user's choices. For instance, eBay is a database driven website: for every query on the site, a web page of results is created from a database. As it is very difficult for an Internet search engine to index this type of website, the information on these websites is not always indexed.

Read the help pages

Just like the majority of people never read the manual of new appliances and miss out on the best features, so 99 per cent of search engine users do not read the help pages or the frequently asked questions (FAQ). Get off to a head start by spending time studying this information, as it will give you insight into the features and effective usage of the search engine. For example, it will tell you how to use Boolean query language, if and how truncation is possible and search engine specific tips.

Switch to the advanced user interface

After you've read all the help pages, flex your muscles and use the advanced search interface instead of the basic one. The advanced search interface gives you far more power to build an effective query, offering filters, limiters and other advanced options. Take some time to understand all the options and you will see that you have more control over what and how you are searching.

It's all in a word

In the good old days of libraries, thesauri and indexing rules would be used to index information consistently. As mentioned earlier, there is no control over what is published on the Web. Therefore, when using a search engine, one needs to construct queries with the writer in mind: how would a web page author have described the topic you are looking for?

This differs from standard information retrieval techniques, where a known and consistent indexing framework can be used to match a query with information. When using search engines, the following barriers may hinder the quality of your search results:

- *Spelling*: If a word can be spelled differently (e.g. UK and US spelling) or can be spelled incorrectly, rest assured that this will be the case on the Web. So when you are looking for an organisation, also look for *organization*.

- *Word endings*: Take into account that the web page you are looking for can use your keywords in singular, plural or as an adjective.

- *Synonyms and acronyms*: Be aware that experts or other well-informed authors may use other terms to describe what you are looking for. You can use a topical dictionary to find synonyms or correct acronyms. Be aware that acronyms can have different meanings, so include a few words of the phrase the acronym stands for. For example, CGI has two different but equally popular meanings: *common gateway interface*, which is used in the computer network environment, and *computer generated images*, which is used in films and graphics.

More focused searching

In order to focus your query through the billions of web pages in search engines, it often helps to frame it:

- Using Google's advanced search options, you can narrow your search to a particular language or country domain. For example, when looking specifically for German web pages, limit your search to the domain '.de'.

- If you can think of an organisation that is related to the topic you are looking for, add that organisation's name to your query. For example, if you are looking for UK unemployment statistics you could add 'Department for Work and Pensions' to your query.

- If you cannot immediately think or a relevant organisation, you can try to find it by adding words like 'institute', 'department', 'association' or 'agency' to your query.

- If you know what type of information you are looking for, add a description to your query, such as 'review', 'test', 'map', 'study', 'report' or 'FAQ'.

- When you have found a relevant organisation, also use the search engine on that website as that may find more appropriate information than a general Internet search engine.

- If you know of words that you do not want included in your results, exclude them with the Boolean NOT operator, often expressed as a minus sign (-).[1] This is especially useful when your search terms have more than one meaning.

Search strategies tutorials

The University of Berkeley Library hosts a very helpful website (*http://www.lib.berkeley.edu/TeachingLib/Guides/Internet/FindInfo.html*) with online guides and tutorials on how to find information on the Internet. The website offers help from starting to analyse a problem, defining a query to selecting and using the appropriate search engine.

Note

1. Readers with a keen eye might note that this symbol is a technically a hyphen, as most books will present a minus sign as '–'. The minus sign is presented here as '-' as this is the symbol that appears on pressing the minus key, and it is the symbol that the search engine will recognise as the minus sign.

4

You see the big picture

When I started working in my first job, one of the best pieces of advice was to 'see the big picture'. By looking outside my own small piece of work and responsibility, and looking at the whole environment of departments, processes, stakeholders and trends, I knew where I wanted to position my department and myself.

In your job as an information professional, be it in a large multinational corporation or as a starting entrepreneur, you will realise that you are part of a bigger puzzle. Often it is hard not to get lost in your daily tasks, or corner of the organisation – but realise our work is part of a bigger scheme. If you understand how the pieces of the puzzle all fit together, you will feel less frustrated with changes in the bigger picture and you will also see more opportunities for your department and yourself. Ultimately, if you can see the big picture, prioritising and making decisions will be easier for you. Based on your view, you know the best options for the 'grand strategy' and you can anticipate trends.

This chapter describes tips and techniques to help you and others see the big picture.

Systems thinking

Systems thinking allows us to understand the bigger picture in our organisation or part of the world, like an engineer understands all the different components and their relationships in a machine in order to fix a problem with a particular part. It is key to recognise that many small tasks, projects and systems are interrelated, and a change in one area can have predicted or unpredicted effects on other parts of the system or organisation.

Instead of breaking up the thing being analysed into smaller pieces, systems thinking focuses on how the thing being analysed interacts in the context of other things. This means taking a holistic view of the interactions of all the different pieces. Especially when a problem is more complex or occurs in a dynamic environment, systems thinking can help achieve far better conclusions.

Below are techniques to stimulate systems thinking:

- *Create a map*: Visualise the overall structure of your problem, team or system.

- *Understand other tasks and projects*: Find out what tasks are being carried out by other departments or project teams that relate to your work – see how they fit with what you do, and whether the priorities in the different project teams or departments are aligned.

- *Try to see the project or department from one level upwards in your organisation*: Talk to people at that level and find out how visible your project or department is and its place in the business strategy – this helps you achieve a high-level view, a view of your part of the world from a higher perspective, seeing the context and relations of your part in a broader context.

- *Gain different perspectives*: Ask colleagues and outsiders their opinion on the problem you are faced with. Either you will find a majority agreeing on a similar point of view, or you will get different points of view. If most people agree with one opinion, you have a clear picture on where to look for a solution. If there are divergent points of view, you can draw a diagram of the different components related to your problem – this will help you take a clearer view and work towards a solution.

Create a map

Use a very large piece of paper to map the total picture as you know it. You can use the topics below as a starter. Start jotting them down on sticky notes for 15 minutes, and then start grouping them. You can use arrows to connect which groups influence one another or are dependent on one another. When you have finished, stand back from the picture and see how you and your department fit in:

- the organisational structure;
- the top five business drivers;
- your organisation's funding model or sources of income;
- the mission statement;
- your organisation's goals;
- the main assets;
- the main processes;
- disciplines;
- stakeholders (internal and external);
- trends in your industry;
- events in the world that influence your organisation.

It is often very valuable to do this exercise with a small team, as you will find out that colleagues will have a different view of these topics. When your big picture is complete, you could also discuss it with a mentor or senior manager to get a higher-level opinion.

The eyes of an outsider

During a team discussion on a new project, strategy or products, you will often tend to view everything from your own perspective. This may block new views or radically different opinions, as these do not fit the current perspective.

In order to help you and your team step outside of your current perspective you can ask the group what an outsider would think. This outsider can be any real or fictitious character, as long as it is well known to the whole team. For example, how would your highest ranking manager react to your new project? A well-known customer? A competitor? A new employee who has just started his first day? By choosing a particular outsider, you can gain a particular perspective or you can chose a random outsider just to change perspectives.

Develop a timeline

If you would like others to appreciate the development of your department or a long lasting project, develop a timeline. Based on events and decisions during that time, depict the timeline on a wall, using pictures, quotes or important moments as illustrations.

Information processing styles

In essence there are two styles how our mind processes information in order to make sense of it: the analytical style and the global style. Both styles are present in our minds, but we all have a natural preference for one of them.

The analytical style has a tendency to focus on the details in information, and then tries putting them together in order to create a sensible picture for us. A disadvantage is that by focusing on the different parts of the problem, this style tends to have difficulty seeing the bigger picture.

Opposed to this, the global style tries to see the bigger picture. It will try to place the information pieces in the wider scope of things to make sense. The disadvantage of this style is that by separating a problem into smaller parts, it can make it harder to solve.

An example of the different styles can be seen in the way people solve jigsaw puzzles. People with a preference for the analytical style will focus on the individual puzzle pieces and how they fit together. They may fit together several pieces and only then look at the picture on the box. The global style will take a more holistic view of the puzzle and select the edge pieces first. Following this, they will look at the picture on the box to see where all the other pieces have to go.

By being aware of your personal information processing style, you can learn whether you have a natural tendency to look at the bigger picture. If you have a preference for the analytical style, remember that this is very effective, so solve problems by splitting them in easier sub-problems. Cooperate with someone who has a global style to become a well-rounded team.

5

You maintain a healthy work–life balance

Like most of us, I sometimes struggle with all the commitments in life: my family, my job, my hobbies, leisure and a social life. Especially as I am ambitious and a perfectionist, I often feel the need to do a lot at the same time – and do it well. This sometimes gives me the feeling I am always one step behind, unsatisfied with the lack of balance between the work and the rest of my activities.

I have learned the hard way to find the right balance between work and the other activities that complete my life. In late 1999, I started to show symptoms of repetitive strain injury (RSI) which was a real problem for me as my job as information manager required me to work with computers every day. At first I tried to suppress and hide the pain, but in early 2000 I could not type a short e-mail without terrible pain in my right hand and arm. I went to see the company doctor who, at that time, did not know much about RSI and its causes. He told me to take more breaks between computer work and do exercises for my arm and hand muscles. This did help a bit, but the pain level kept rising. I was lucky that someone referred me to a physiotherapist who explained to me that this pain was my body's way of saying 'watch out, you are not in balance – this is no longer healthy'.

Besides a physical treatment to help me ease the pain and learn how to work with computers in a correct and ergonomical way, I was also sent to a counsellor. At first I was not sure why I needed to see him as my problem was physical. However, he made me realise that my life was out of balance, which caused high levels of stress and anxiety. Because of these stress levels I was always tensed, never really giving myself time to relax which caused my muscles to become too cramped. So, to fix my RSI, I had to learn how to work more ergonomically and also get my life in balance. And to be honest – that was one of the hardest things I had ever done. I had to learn not to worry about work 24/7, learn how to enjoy a hobby, not feel guilty when I said no to a request and in general get my life priorities in order.

The 'right' balance in your life is very personal and will change for each of us at different times in our lives. The good news is that I finally found my balance, and if I can do it, so can you!

Below are tips and ideas to help you find your work–life balance.

Technology intrusion

While we are seeking a balance between work and family, the advances in technology intrude in our personal lives: think of cell phones, Web access, e-mail and laptop computers all bringing work into our personal lives. Even when we are away from the office, we are still connected to it by a cord of technology.

Use technology to work more flexibly – not to work more and longer. If you have a family commitment during the afternoon, use a laptop and your home Internet connection to make up for the missed time in the evening. Or dial into teleconferences from your quiet den at home, instead of driving all the way to the office – saving the commuting time.

Telecommuting

Ever since 2001 I have been telecommuting for one day per week, and I find this to be a very useful way to balance my work and life. My manager benefits from a better motivated, more productive employee and I have one day per week to actually get things done. Based on my experiences, there are some key success factors you, your colleagues and your boss need to consider when you think about telecommuting:

- *Commitment*: Your colleagues, your boss, your family and yourself need to be committed to telecommuting. It comes down to establishing trust for all parties. Your boss and colleagues need to trust that you will be equally or even more productive from home. You need to trust them that they will keep you in the loop when you are working from home. Gain that trust by agreeing on set days or times when your will telecommute, how and when you will be in touch, and planning meetings that physically require you to be in the office. Your family also needs to understand when you are working and thus not available for them.

- *Communication and cooperation*: Everyone should agree how you will communicate when you are telecommuting and what hardware and software is needed, for example, a laptop, mobile phone, access to the corporate computer network and the Internet.

- *Work culture*: If the culture is focused on self-managing, and professional teams that set their own targets, telecommuting should be fairly easy. If you have a manager that only feels you are productive when they see you, you need to bring that to the table.

- *Project phase*: If you are working on projects, the early phases (forming, storming and norming according to Tuckerman, 1965) are usually those that require face-to-face meetings. This because they are very interactive and also establish the trust between project members. If the project has started and the team members know each other and know who will do what and when, telecommuting is ideal.

- *Self-discipline*: This is essential when you are telecommuting. You need to be able to plan your own work and stick to your own planning. Be strict with yourself when you will stop working, as it is often tempting to 'go that extra mile' in the evening (or sometimes at night). You need a balance between work and your own life, as telecommuting often blurs that distinction.

Part-time work or job sharing

If you want to spend less time working, but do not want to quit your job, consider working part-time or sharing your job with a colleague. Find out if there are official policies about this in your organisation and set up a discussion with your manager and HR adviser. Before doing this, have a clear story in mind why you want to do this and how you see this working, for example, in the area of continuity.

A high-level view of your life

Try to stand back from your life, as if you were hovering above your life, to see what commitments you have to balance. One way of doing this is keeping a journal of how you spent your time over a week or two. Then group all the activities into the main groups of money, health, relationships and self-development. See how much time you spend on each of these groups and whether you feel that is in balance with the other groups. You will then see how your balance is currently and can compare this with how you would want it to be.

Mentoring

A mentor is a very good way to cope with your work–life balance. By approaching this trusted person, you can share your problems and discuss how you feel. Your mentor can help you reflect on your life and the issues that you are facing. Just knowing that someone is available who can act as a sounding board and help to find solutions to your problems is a relief. Perhaps your organisation already has a mentoring programme, if not, you may find a mentor through an information professional organisation or your personal network.

Build a safety net

Your partner, your parents or a close friend know you better than you know yourself. Ask them how they see the way you live your live – especially the way you balance all your life commitments. They can give you an honest view and advice, often building on their own experiences.

Learn to say 'no'

See Chapter 12 on time management and saying 'no' to help you learn how you can get better at this.

Think positively

If you tend to worry a lot, try to bring a positive spin to a situation or problem. Things could always be much worse, and most of the time, things will turn out less bad than you had imagined. Write down what you worry about, and what you think the effects will be. Very often, just putting it on paper creates a distance between you and the problem. You can also confide in a mentor or a partner, which not only helps you get things off your chest, but also provides you with a sounding board. Others will be able to rationalise your worries and help you see reality.

Release the inner child

This may sound a bit weird, but sometimes we should give into to things we enjoyed when we were kids. Remember the fun you had when you were young? Relive those times by just having plain, simple fun: have a snowball fight, kick leaves during autumn, play with a miniature racetrack or climb a tree. Especially when you have children (or can 'borrow' them), this is a great opportunity to relieve stress.

Learn from the best

Do you know of someone you admire who seems to have found that ideal work–life balance? If it is possible, try and meet them to discuss their experiences and lessons learned. They may have been in a similar situation and can help you out.

Exercise

Especially if you work in an office, make sure you get enough exercise to train your body – sitting behind a desk and working on computers all day simply does not give your body the exercise it needs. In addition, exercising also helps you to keep your mind away from work and worries. So find out what exercise you prefer, be it walking, working out at the gym, yoga or tennis and make it a habit.

Take a career break

If you would like to get away from your work for a while to find out what you really want to do with your life, you may want to consider taking a sabbatical leave. Larger organisations often have formal policies about sabbaticals, so contact your HR adviser about this. Other, smaller, organisations will not have formal policies but may be open for a good business case. Do think twice before you start talking about this with your manager:

- Do you know why you want a sabbatical?
- How much time do you need?
- What do you want to achieve during that period away from work?
- Do you want to return to the same job ... or even the same employer?
- How will you sell this idea to your manager, i.e. what is in it for them?

The sabbatical can be used to travel around the world, do community work, spend more time with family or simply do what you want. Perhaps you want to learn how to play the guitar, sculpt or even write a book!

Sleep

In order to cope with your normal busy day, it is essential that you get enough sleep. You will know yourself well enough to estimate how much hours of sleep per night you need to function properly. I have found out that the older I get, the more I need a good night of sleep. The days of staying up until the early hours, taking a few hours of sleep and still coping with a full day of commitments are, unfortunately, over.

- *Limit alcohol and caffeine*: Avoid drinking caffeinated or alcoholic beverages a few hours before bedtime.

- *Don't exercise before bedtime*: Exercise will stimulate your body, interfering with your ability to sleep.

- *Develop a regular schedule*: If possible with your family and work, go to bed and wake up at the same time every day, including the weekends. This will help your body know when to sleep at the same time each day.

- *Relax before going to bed*: Read a magazine, a book, listen to relaxing music or do relaxation exercises.

- *Put down your worries*: If you lie awake, worrying about all kinds of problems in your life – write them down. Just the fact that you have written them down may already ease your mind.

6

You show leadership

Very often, leadership is considered to be the same as management. The simplest difference between those two terms is that you can be appointed a manager, but can only become a leader. A manager can only be effective when management techniques are complemented by leadership skills.

If you are not a manager, you can still be a leader – being a leader is about being able to influence teams to work towards a common goal. As a leader, you do not have employees but followers, who believe in your leadership to actually 'lead the way'. There are many different kinds of leadership, and each of us should be able to find a style that fits us.

As an information professional, you can be a leader in the information management discipline, in your organisation or your community. In my career I have had the good luck to work with several leaders who have influenced my work and personality. A good leader inspires you to do great things and facilitates the road towards a particular goal.

One example of a very inspiring leader in my case was Geert Kobus, a pioneer in the area of semantic networks, linguistic technology and taxonomies.

I met him in 2002 when his company helped me with a pilot project to evaluate brand new automatic classification software. Not only was Geert a guru in his field, he was also able to transfer his enthusiasm for the project to all participants. Always the one with a positive spin on problems and a totally honest personality, Geert literally drove the project to a success just by sharing his vision, making others enthusiastic and giving project participants freedom to achieve their goals.

In addition to his business activities, he was also very interested in using technology to help lesser developed areas of our world. Part of his company's profit was donated to charity and Geert networked with other technology companies to start projects in Africa to help them build a better future. Although he was always working on new ideas, he never ceased to enjoy the good life: good conversations, a well placed joke and spending time with his family was his counterbalance to his busy work routine.

At the end of the project I was not only very satisfied with the outcome of the project, I also felt inspired by Geert's leadership – I clearly saw how new technologies would shape the future for information professionals and I learned that being successful in life also means enjoying yourself.

Sadly, Geert passed away soon after our project was finished, much too soon. One of the lessons he taught me was not to postpone pursuing my dreams. The result of one of those dreams is now in your hands: I had always wanted to write a book, but always postponed it due to lack of time. His passing away was the trigger for me to bring more balance into my life by pursuing my dreams in business and in my personal life.

Building leadership competency

Being a leader is a competency that is gained over time. In this chapter I have gathered insights and techniques to help you expand your leadership capabilities.

Leading by example

In order to be accepted as a leader, you must not only 'talk the talk', but also 'walk the talk'. People will judge you not just by your words, but mostly by your actions. If you do not set the right example, why would others? Be aware that giving the bad example will create a longer lasting impression than a good example.

Take a critical look at what you stand for, what you say and how you have given good examples. You could ask a mentor to reflect on your leadership by example, as this is a quality that should be nurtured over time.

Learn from the best

Who are the leaders you admire? Look around in your organisation and network for people that show leadership you can learn from. Study how they express their leadership and what you can take away from these examples. If you have a leader in your direct network, you can approach them for guidance. Especially in trade associations like the American Library Association (ALA), the Special Library Association (SLA) and the Chartered Institute of Library and Information Professionals (CILIP), more experienced leaders are open to share their qualities and experiences with others who would like to learn.

Enthusiasm

Nothing is more contagious than enthusiasm. If you encounter someone who is clearly excited about a new idea and simply radiates enthusiasm, it is hard to resist sharing that enthusiasm. Enthusiasm helps others to build willingness to change, to work harder, cooperate, study or make decisions. You can stimulate enthusiasm by telling others what the ideal solution would be, what it takes to get there and how people will feel when the ideal solution is reached. Genuinely describe how you feel about the proposed solution, why it makes you feel good and interact with people to share those feelings and build enthusiasm.

Training courses and workshops

As leadership is seen as an important characteristic for information professionals nowadays, there is a wide variety of leadership training courses and workshops. Your own organisation may have a learning curriculum, or the trade association you belong to will have opportunities for you to study leadership. Interactive courses or workshops where you can practise your leadership capabilities are especially valuable. By attending a course or workshop you will also meet others who are expanding their leadership skills – an excellent opportunity for your network.

Communication

Communication is the most critical, but also the most often neglected and undervalued characteristic of a good leader. Be open. Listen to others. Ask questions. Consult your employees, colleagues, managers, outside experts. Make people feel involved with decisions. Explain reasons why things are the way they are. Explain why things should change – and how. Even if you do not have all the information, never hold back on communication but explain what you do know.

Trust

If you are leading others, trust them to do as you have agreed – give them time and space to do it their way. Let them gain your trust by showing results but achieving them in their own way. Try and steer the outcome of people's actions, rather than the way they achieve the outcome. If you are a perfectionist like me, you will find it hard that others do not do things as you would. I sometimes restrain myself from trying to help other people, as I know trusting them will mean better results in the long term. If you do not trust others to perform their work, they will become frustrated and unmotivated.

Be trusted

Giving trust and gaining trust are linked capabilities for a leader. Like you trust others, you will have to gain their trust. As a manager, for example, your team members should be able to trust you to represent their interests in management meetings. Trust is something that can only be gained in a relationship over time, it can not be switched on.

Here are some tips on gaining trust:

- *Reflective listening:* Let the other person talk and then tell them back what you understood. Humans are different from computers, so our communication is often more fuzzy and less to the point. So rephrase what the other person said until both of you conclude you have 'got it'.

- *Ask questions*: Be interested in what is going on in other people's lives and jobs. Not only will you learn a lot, others will also feel that you are interested in them.

- *Follow up on your promises*: Like your mother always said: do not make a promise you cannot keep. Even if it would be easier to make that promise and try and get away with not keeping it, that particular act will remain long in people's minds.

- *Take responsibility*: As a leader, take your responsibility when it is required. Explain clearly when something is not your responsibility, but never shy away from taking what is dutifully yours.

- *Ask for the truth*: It is better knowing the truth than not knowing it, as not knowing means you cannot act upon it. This might be one of the hardest things to do, as the truth sometimes can be hard and painful. Let others know that you always want to them to give you the truth and not a version of the truth.

- *Give credit for achievements and successes*: Give credit to the team and the individual to build trust and team spirit. Do not take all the credit, as achievements as a leader are not solely your effort – were it not for others, you would not have achieved that success – nor would you be a leader.

- *Change your point of view and explain why*: If you have a point of view, there surely will be times when that will change due to new experiences or information. Like everyone, you are entitled to change your mind – but explain why.

- Lastly, but surely the most important is *giving trust*. Trust is a two-way street.

Challenge everything

If you have young children, you know the period in their lives when they keep asking 'why?' They start by asking simple questions and then ask 'why' for your every answer: 'Why do cars drive on the road?' 'Otherwise they would collide with the pedestrians' 'Why?' And so on. Kids are curious by nature and do not accept things just because. That curious nature is still inside our adult selves and should be used more often. We will often feel that asking 'why' will make others think we are not smart or 'don't get it'. Wrong. Challenge established procedures or new ideas by asking 'why' a couple of times after every explanation. It is very illuminating to see how easy it is to get to the bottom of things.

Celebrate

If there is a reason for celebration – use it! We work hard and tend to focus on what went wrong, or only talk about what should have been done better. As a leader you can break that cycle and pick out the reasons for celebration. A few examples:

- You could have a public announcement of highlights every month on the intranet or during a team meeting.
- When a colleague or employee has done something outstanding, perhaps you can get top management to write a thank-you note.
- If a project has been finished on time, invite all project members for drinks or create a nice award to remind them of their achievement.

By celebrating, you will not only lighten up everyone's day but also make all involved feel proud and more energised.

Take time to think

We all know that life often feels like rushing by, leaving us little time to reflect and think. As a leader you need to disconnect from your hectic work routine and busy life to think about your plans and ideas. Only if you do this will you be able to look at your work with a fresh eye and give your mind a chance to come up with new ideas or refreshing insights.

You may want to read the chapter on work–life balance for more ideas to find time to think and let the creativity start flowing.

Mentor and be mentored

As a leader, you can help other by being a guide and teacher in their life. Based on your insights and experience, you can help others cope with their challenges and provide a fresh view.

Even perhaps as a more experienced and senior information professional you can benefit from a mentor. A mentor can help you reflect on how you perceive your career and the possible decisions you have to take. By being mentored and providing mentoring to others, you can keep growing as a person and a leader.

Making things happen

My grandfather started out as a carpenter; his work was making things like tables, chairs or cupboards – things that you could see and touch.

When growing as a leader, most information professional jobs are more about making things happen, rather than actually producing something tangible. Compare the task of cataloguing a book with a project that should encourage more diversity in your department. Cataloguing a book deals with an actual book and a catalogue, both of which you can see and touch. The end result is also something you can see in your mind before starting, and you can easily determine the steps how to catalogue. At the end, the result is something you and others can see.

When your job includes more management tasks, they will focus less on tangible tasks but more on 'making things happen'. It is harder to imagine what the end result will look like and how to achieve that result. As a leader, you can use the following rules to 'make things happen':

- What is the goal you want to reach? Can you envision it? What would success look or feel like?

- Build a story for your team members to explain the goal.

- How would you measure success?

- Can you break down the plan to achieve the goal in steps?

- Define who should take part in the team to achieve the goal. Rather than naming people, describe the roles and requirements.

- Get everyone in the team committed to the goal and their particular objectives.

- It is then your duty as a leader to enable your team members to achieve their objectives – provide resources, time and motivation.

Be available

Very often I will feel too busy to be available to others. If I feel there are too many demands on my time, I will lock myself in a different room not to be disturbed by others. I will explain to my team members why I do this and how I will be available – for urgent matters and that I will join them for lunch or coffee. People need to know when you will be available and how – as long as they know that, they will be able to come to you when they need you.

Trust your intuition – but validate it

There have been many discussions in management literature on the value of intuition. Even though we have learned to take rational decisions, based on numbers and thorough understanding, our intuition is usually correct. Listen to that intuition – but validate it. Find supporting information for your intuition and take the decision. Often you do not need 100 per cent of the information to make that decision – the decision will be no different if you only have 80 per cent of the information and that last 20 per cent of information may take too long to gather, meanwhile the opportunity will have passed.

7

You can persuade others

As an information professional you will have to convince your management, your colleagues or customers about your ideas. Whether it be the case that you want to upgrade a software application, adopt a new strategy for your department or implement an organisation-wide project – you will need to persuade others. Simply put, persuasion is the way of changing someone else's point of view or behaviour to your own.

Persuasion is a game we all play on different levels every day. Commercials and advertisements use persuasion to sell products. At home, we use persuasion with our family to influence our loved ones to go and see the movie we like or eat at that restaurant we really like.

For the Ancient Greeks, the ideal method of persuasion was to use reasoning alone, which they named *logos* – the appeal to reason. They understood that humans do not follow reason alone, but that other persuasion techniques should be used as well: the appeal to character (*ethos*) and the appeal to emotion (*pathos*).

By combining logos, ethos and pathos you can define the optimal mix of persuasion techniques for a particular situation. In this chapter, I will describe different techniques you can use to persuade others.

Persuasion is close to coercion, as they both aim to change the other person's attitude or behaviours. But where coercion uses fear and intimidation, persuasion refers to more positive methods by using emotional or rational appeals based on common values and understandings (Pruitt, 1986).

Techniques

By using persuasion you apply reasoning, urging or convincing to get others to change their behaviour or point of view. In order to motivate others to the best effect, you must use different persuasive techniques, such as the following.

Understand other people's interests

With every new idea, people always think 'what's in it for me?' Your idea might be very logical, but bear in mind that people usually put their own interests first – their personal interest, the interest for their team or organisation. Be aware of this, and look at your idea from the other side. What benefits can you offer people to persuade them?

For example, early in my career I had to convince the general manager of the company I worked for to implement a web-enabling module for our library catalogue which contained our library collection and customer files.

This meant a significant investment in times when IT spending was declining and the acquisition of new software was challenged every time. I knew, however, that the general manager was very keen on making all employees work more efficiently. The board of directors had set several targets for him in this respect, and the general manager was always looking for proposals in the area.

So when I put together a short proposal for the investment, I referred to his efficiency programme and explained how all employees now had one-click access to all relevant customer information. Rather than going to the library about a customer file or specific letter, employees could now easily search and browse the catalogue and access it immediately. The vendor was able to deliver a case study of another company, where the implementation of the module was a great success regarding efficiency.

So rather then seeing my proposal as just a cost, the general manager saw it as an investment in making the company work more efficiently and enabling him to score on his targets.

Expertise

Expertise is a convincing factor in persuasion, as people tend to be influenced by experts on topics they know less about. When we want to read a book on a certain topic, we select the book not just by the content, but also by the author's credentials.

Knowing you have expertise also makes you feel more confident, as you have the knowledge and are prepared for questions or issues. Of course, it takes quite some time and effort to acquire expertise. Identify experts in your organisation or industry and learn from them, and make sure you are up to date with the latest developments via courses, journals and conferences. You can gain recognition as an expert on a topic by expressing your ideas in articles, giving advice or presenting papers at conferences.

Show you can be trusted

If someone you do not trust tries to persuade you, it is very unlikely they will succeed. Make sure people believe that you are sincere and can be trusted. First of all, this can be done by stating your accomplishments and expertise: your successes, your credentials and references from others. Second, use your expertise to show you know what you are talking about. Last, but not least, trust is gained by proving you understand your audience's situation.

Be enthusiastic

If you are enthusiastic about an idea, this often rubs off on your audience. Explain why you are so enthusiastic about your idea and why they should be as well. However, be aware that the level of enthusiasm should not be over-the-top. When someone is considered to be too enthusiastic about something, the trustworthiness often decreases.

Use persuasive words to convey your message

By using certain words in your presentation or discussion, you can appeal to people's emotions (Leeds, 2003). For example:

- *New*: This appeals to people's desires for something new, something different.

- *Easy*: In essence, we all want everything to be easy. Especially if your idea sounds complicated, explain how easy it is.

- *Guarantee*: People tend to avoid risks. New ideas potentially carry risks, so it is good to guarantee that the perceived risk is either not there or can be mitigated.

- *Results*: You should be explicit about what your idea or project will deliver.

Provide third-party evidence

You can refer to other organisations who have already implemented your idea, or research reports that support your point of view. If the evidence comes from trusted sources like industry organisations, well-known journals or industry leaders the evidence is especially compelling.

Summarise and analyse

During a discussion of your new idea or project, listen to the input of others and work it into a logical conclusion in favour of your idea. Some people can immediately be in favour of your idea, but others may show hesitation. Analyse the reasons for hesitation and think of mitigation for them, which you can work into a logical summary. Start by restating the support you got and summarise how you will address the hesitations that have been voiced.

Firm statements

Practise your pitch with colleagues or a relative. You have to express belief in your idea, both by your choice of words, the tone of your voice and body language. When you want to persuade others, make eye contact with participants, sound calm and firm as if your idea is the best. Your voice should be calm and without hesitation, which you can achieve by practising and asking feedback from others.

Start off with a statement regarding your idea: what problem it will solve, the results it will deliver or how it will save costs. Outline how you will achieve this and recognise risks or uncertainties – but immediately address them, taking away hesitations. At the end of your presentation or discussion, summarise what you have said and be clear on what you want from others. Analyse how 30-second television commercials use body language, choice of words and tone to persuade you.

Request a favour

In general, people are helpful and will not immediately respond negatively when being asked a favour. When you present your idea, appeal to people's good side and ask for their help or support. When they like your idea, people are especially likely to respond to a request for a favour. Make clear how their favour would help you and appeal to their good Samaritan side: 'If I could have five minutes of your valuable time to fill out this questionnaire, that would really help me out'.

Reward

If you want other to change their behaviour or ideas, a reward is a powerful instrument. Remember how your parents rewarded you for doing something you did not like? You thought of that new bike you would get for your birthday while you mowed the grass every Saturday afternoon. Even when we are grown-ups, rewards can be used to persuade us: be it a bonus, a compliment or promise to support our promotion.

Use humour

John Cleese once said: 'If I can get you to laugh with me, you like me better, which makes you more open to my ideas. And if I can persuade you to laugh at the particular point I make, by laughing at it you acknowledge its truth.'

Humour puts people in a good mood and can relieve tension during meetings. If it fits your style, you can use humour to be more effective in communication. It will reduce people's initial resistance to the message or point you are trying to get across. Make sure that the humour you use is relevant to the situation, as bad humour or badly timed humour will backfire.

Step in the other person's shoes

In order to persuade someone else, you should understand the situation from their point of view. Pretend you are that other person, based on the information you have gained so far and your personal experiences. If you were the other person, what would your opinion be? What would be your questions and concerns? Perhaps you know someone who is in a similar position or job, they could provide insights to how the other person thinks and feels.

If you have known the other person for a while, be open about this: tell them you want to understand their views, their concerns and opinions. Explain that this will help you help them better, and in the long run everyone will benefit.

Based on those insights, you can then better judge the situation and decide what your actions should be.

Both sides of the story

When trying to persuade someone, outline both the pros and cons of your ideas. This will make you look fair and more objective. As we all know, there is no such thing as total objectivity – but you can use this technique to take away concerns and uneasy feelings. Emphasise the pros and explain how the cons can be mitigated. Finally, every situation will have benefits and drawbacks – so explain how the benefits will outweigh the drawbacks.

Say you want to convince your manager to permit you to take a one-week training course on project management skills. The benefit is that you will return from the training well-equipped to run projects and your general value for the organisation has increased. The drawback is that you will be away from your job for a week, and your manager may worry you will be lured away by a competitor now that he has just paid for your training. In this case, you have 'read his mind' and you can weigh up the pros and cons. Convince him that you have agreed with your co-workers what to do with your day-to-day work and that you will check your voicemail every day. Describe what projects you will be able to take on when you return, which will benefit the department and organisation. Finally, tell him you would appreciate his approval of the training as you feel that this training will contribute to your future career in the organisation.

8

You are an effective networker

In our networked society, having a good network of contacts is essential to be successful, but as information professionals we have an advantage: it is an insider secret that librarians and information professionals are among the nicest people in the world.

Over the years, I have been amazed at how often a fellow librarian will go out of their way to share their experience or provide great help to me. I think this can be tracked to one of our core values as information professionals which is all about helping people. This is a very powerful characteristic, which makes us stronger as a professional group.

In essence, networking is the art of meeting and building long-lasting connections with people who can be of help to you and who you could help in return.

I experienced the power of a good network last year during a high-profile project in which I was involved. My organisation had hired an outside consultancy firm to scrutinise all services related to information management with two goals in mind:

- create a plan to globalise all these services, which were then all regionally or locally focused and funded;
- find cost savings by globalising these services.

Besides library services, other information management services like helpdesks, archives and web design were also part of the study. This enormous study was split into different groups, each focusing on a different set of related services. I was one of the leaders of the library services group, tasked with building a plan to globalise the more than 30 different library locations around the world. One of the first phases in the project was a benchmarking study, to measure on a global scale where our library services were positioned, compared with our peers in other multinational organisations.

Using the professional network I had built up over the years, I was quickly able to identify good benchmarking partners for this study. As one of the very few groups in our globalisation study, we had a good number of benchmarking partners who were willing to share their global library experiences, numbers and strategies with us in confidence. Some of these contacts were librarians I had only met virtually via e-mails or chat sessions, so I was once again impressed by the willingness of my library peers to help out.

During the project review, our group was praised for our benchmarking phase – especially our capabilities of finding very good benchmarking partners who shared great insights into their library best practices.

Networking tips

In the following pages I will share useful tips to build a successful network, which will be essential in your career. You can use your network to build new business, build alliances, seek expertise, to find a new job or a candidate for a job opening.

Who are you looking for?

Know what kind of contacts you are looking for at a venue – this makes identifying them easier. However, do not close off contacts that do not immediately match the profile you are looking for. You could ask people you meet if they know someone who might be interested in helping you or whom you could help out: 'Sounds like your colleague is having a lot of troubles getting the document management system organised. Like I said, I have quite some experience in that – feel free to give her my details, I'd be glad to share tips and helpful training guides.'

What's in a name?

The very first thing to do when meeting someone, is to shake hands and repeat their name. This will make it easier for you to remember that name, as your memory will now connect their face to that name. If you haven't understood their name properly, you will also be corrected and you can remember the correct name and pronunciation.

About yourself

Prepare a description of yourself, your work and organisation that can be said in a two or three sentences. This is often refered to as an 'elevator speech'; for instance: 'Hi, I am David Hungate, and I am the head librarian for the chemicals division of the Toto Corporation. My main responsibilities include the development of an electronic content strategy and digital preservation of our historic business records.' This introduction explains who you are, what you do, where you work and what your work includes. People now have the chance to react to one or more pieces of information in your introduction.

Starting a conversation

One of the most difficult things is starting a conversation with a stranger. As a conversation starter, look for an easy opener. If you are both at a company meeting, you can ask what department they are in; if you meet someone during a conference, you can start by commenting on an interesting presentation you have seen – there is always something to start that conversation. And you know what? Most people will be glad you were the one who started talking.

During your first meeting, look for common ground: organisations you both have worked for, college, professional associations, place of birth, hobbies or type of work.

Make notes

When you first meet people, you will gain a lot of information about them. Make it a habit to keep notes regarding the person you met, for instance, on the back of their business card or in your PDA. Later, those few keywords will remind you who you met and potentially what any follow-up action should be.

College network

If you are in college, start building a network there with fellow students and teachers. These are the days when it is relatively easy to start networking, as everyone is at the start of their professional life. This is a network that you can tap into for the rest of your life.

If your college has an alumni organisation, do join them:

■ you have easy access to your old college classmates but also more senior information professionals who are just an e-mail or phone call away;

- alumni organisations will hold reunions, an excellent opportunity to network;
- access or participate as an online mentor in virtual groups of alumni who share their professional and educational experiences;
- often you can participate in online discussion forums and meet with professors during live chats;
- remember when you are further down the career path to help out the new graduates!

Other networks

Below is a short list of events or groups with a networking aim. Make sure you attend a number of events, also outside your profession, to maximise your network opportunities:

- chambers of commerce;
- sport events;
- conferences and workshops;
- trade and professional association meetings;
- vendor events;
- community organisations.

In the age of the Internet, networking also has a virtual dimension. Through online discussion forums, e-mail lists, web communities or social networks (like LinkedIn or Friendster) time and place no longer play a role for networking. You can network with people in different time zones and continents, who may be very relevant for your network. Find out through online directories, your colleagues or professional organisation what the most suitable online tools are for you.

Show interest in everyone

You have to show interest in everyone you meet, which is a skill you can develop.

In college I had a professor who was a master in this skill. He could enter a room of strangers and have lively conversations with people he had never met, with totally different backgrounds and careers. His secret was that he was genuinely interested in everybody and everything, which he showed by truly listening and asking questions.

You will not know upfront what people's expertise or background is, so ask people questions that make them talk to find out more about themselves.

Use generic questions to start the conversation and pick up on clues in people's answers. For instance: 'how did you get started in the business of ... ?', 'what are the biggest challenges you have faced in your career?' or 'who influenced you most during your career?' Make sure you are not firing off questions so people feel forced to talk, keep looking for verbal and non-verbal signals when to stop asking.

Keep in touch and surprise people

Building a network is just the start of networking – you will also have to maintain it. There is a variety of options to stay in touch, you should choose the ways that are appropriate to use with a specific contact.

You can stay in touch by updating your contacts via an e-mail about something that you think might be of interest to them. It can be a link to a website, a short piece of information you heard or an update on your project. And as real mail (the paper version) is almost becoming extinct in the twenty-first century, sending a handwritten postcard or note on a special occasion can make someone's day. If you know of special occasions or moments in someone's life, use these to get in touch. Of course, a birthday is the most well-known occasion, but there are other moments where you can get in touch. For example, your peer in another part of the organisation cancels a meeting because it is her son's graduation – pick up the phone and congratulate her! It's simple and it will mean a lot to them.

Salespeople

Even though the relationship with a salesperson is sometimes considered to be only commercial, I find it very useful to include them in my network. Instead of only wanting to sell you a service or a product, salespeople nowadays want to be partners and develop long relationships with you. Naturally, the commercial element will always be present, but do remember that salespeople network for a living. Through them you will be able to get introduced to other information professionals they know.

If you get invited to vendor events, use this not just to learn about the latest releases, but also to meet peers. It is very easy to start talking during such an event, all you have to ask is to introduce yourself and ask 'I am here to learn how product X can help me achieve Y, what about you?'

To make it even easier, just before the event or at the start, meet with your account manager or sales rep and ask them which other attendees might be relevant for you to meet. They will be very happy to introduce you and off you go!

Pave the way

Pave the way for a follow-up. If you meet an interesting person with whom you'd like to talk further, ask for a follow-up meeting or permission to call at a later time. This can be a telephone call to discuss a mutual goal you want to discuss or a lunch to talk further about how to solve a certain problem. People will be more receptive for a follow-up meeting when you first meet them, than when they have returned to their normal (busy) work routine.

Conferences

Conferences are one of the best networking places for information professionals, with several options to make contact with peers, gurus and other interesting people.

Before attending a conference, virtual discussion forums and mailing lists will often have messages from people who you might like to meet in real life. Spend some time before a conference to make virtual contact with people, who you can then arrange to meet face-to-face at the conference.

Large conferences will often have a list of attendants which you can browse to find out who you might want to meet. Usually there is a noticeboard to put up requests to meet with people for lunch.

Make it a habit to make contact with one stranger every session. This can easily be the person in the seat next to you, before or after a session.

Solicit feedback

When you need to write an article, a short piece for the intranet or your resumé, ask one or more contacts to provide feedback. This will give you a different opinion and very often very good comments to improve your writing.

For example, I usually ask a few people within my network to comment on my articles before finalising them to get their comments on how useful the article is seen through other people's eyes. Especially when I am very knowledgeable on a subject, I tend to forget that my audience needs a good introduction to the topic. Feedback from others points this out for me and I get suggestions how to improve this.

A nice side effect is that you build trust with the contacts from whom you have requested feedback – they feel pride that you have asked them for their opinion.

Join a professional organisation

For professional organisations, networking is a top priority. Find out what type of people you would like to network with, and find out which professional organisations would be able to join that network. This can be a national library association, a trade association or a group of new professionals.

Professional organisations will make your networking easy by online membership directories, divisions or chapters based on interest, online discussion forums, conferences and best practice sharing communities.

Visibility

You can also increase the number of people who would like to network with you by becoming more visible inside and outside your organisation. You can gain visibility by writing, speaking, sharing and in general trying to be a leader in the information management community.

This topic is explored in more detail in Chapter 6 on leadership and Chapter 16 on marketing yourself.

9

You know how you can add value

As an information professional you are in the business of providing services to your customers, and sooner or later you will be adding value. Basically, you add value when you help improve your organisation's return on its investment. Do not confuse value with cost-effectiveness, as the word *value* does not only mean the monetary value but also the subjective perception of the users. I will explain this in more depth later in this chapter.

In essence, your customers should be able to reach their own goals better by using your products and services. In addition, it is very important that you or your department are seen as valuable to the success of the organisation. This means you will have to focus on providing value-added services.

If you add value, it means that the steps you take in the process increase the value of the raw product. For example, as an information professional you can provide essential financial information on potential customers and target markets to sales managers. They will use this information to create a more attractive proposal, and the chances that this will lead to new business are increased.

The flipside of the value coin is cost. For every step in the process, there are costs for your organisation. In this example, it is the time of your searching and editing, plus the costs of the query in commercial databases. In order to survive as an information professional, the increased value should be higher than your costs.

Creating value-added services and proving their value often sounds harder than it usually is. The rest of this chapter describes how you can create value-added services and how you can demonstrate this value to others.

How customers see value

First of all, I'd like to introduce you to the concept of perceived value. This is the value of your services as your customers see it. You can add value to your services not only by directly changing what you deliver, but by changing your customers' perceptions.

Remember that if your customer does not see the value, there is no added value for the organisation.

The perceived value may be different from the actual value, but understanding it is key if you want to be in business. For example, the actual costs for setting up a personalised search alert will be low, but the perceived value for the customer can be quite high – especially if by getting highly relevant information delivered to their mailbox they now have to spend less time on information gathering.

The value of a service or product is derived from four different components:

- *Feature*: A feature is a prominent or characteristic aspect of a product or service. For example, a feature of a personalised search service is the delivery of search alerts.

- *Benefit*: A benefit is what the user gets from the product or service. Benefits are often linked to specific features, but that is not always necessary. Benefits are perceived, not necessarily real. A benefit of a personalised search service is the delivery of targeted, highly relevant information right to the customer's mailbox.

- *Value*: The value is the positive quality that the product or service has for the customer's business. For example, by subscribing to a personalised search service, customers save time (and often frustration) looking for information.

- *Sacrifice*: This is what the customer has to give in return to get the product or service. Usually this is money, but it can also be something else, such as the time for an interview with the information professional to provide input for the personalised search service.

A customer will (un)consciously always weigh value against the sacrifices of a product or service before buying. So you must make sure that the sacrifice is as low as possible, or at least perceived to be as low as possible, and that the value is high or perceived as high.

By working closely with customers, you can gain valuable insight into what they see as the value and sacrifice of your products and services. If you have been turned down by a customer for a specific service, find out if this is related to the value and sacrifice. For example, I once set up a website where customers could search a citation database themselves, using an online questionnaire. After a few weeks, hardly anybody had used it, so I asked several key customers for their reasons. They found the service to be useful, but filling out the form took them more time (sacrifice) than just e-mailing the library with a request for a citation search.

Creating value-added services and products

If you want to focus on delivering value-added services and products, you should characterise each of your activities in your department. Based on this you will see where the real value-added lies and which no-value or lesser-value activities should be examined more closely.

Key to the core business

These are the activities that lie the closest to the core business or primary process of your organisation. It is clear to everyone that your activities are tied directly to the success of the organisation. Quality or customer satisfaction would suffer if these activities were not performed. Understand the value of them and see if you can work more efficiently to provide them, and focus promotion on these types of services or products.

Business value added

These activities are not directly linked to the core business, but are necessary to keep the organisation working. Often these are activities 'that have to be done' for governmental or contractual reasons, like keeping audit trails of files or producing annual reports. Very often, these activities can be very time-consuming and keep you from doing real value-added activities. Scrutinise each of the business value-added activities and find out if they are still needed. In addition, are you most appropriate person or department to perform them?

Low or no value added

The kind of activity that adds little or no value you should consider either stopping, automating or outsourcing. In a library or archive environment, think of activities related to storage and physical retrieval, or straightforward data entry. When you find this hard to accomplish, make a list of these activities and discuss them with your management. State that you want to focus your resources on value-added activities, but low- or no-value activities still consume x percentage of your resources.

If some of the low- or no-value activities have to be done, investigate whether you can automate or outsource them. This way, the activity still continues but for a lower price and not keeping you away from more value-added work.

Examine all your personal and departmental activities regularly, say, every year, to keep you focused on value-added activities.

When you have a good overview of all your activities and their level of value-add, it is time to enhance the value of your services and products with some of the following.

Lowering your prices

If you lower your prices, the sacrifice for the customer to acquire your product or service decreases. If the benefits are perceived as the same before you lowered your prices, this means that the customers' perception of the value has increased.

What you lose by lowering your prices, you can make up with higher volumes. Very often, you will also be able to decrease your costs when you have higher volumes. For instance, when you lower the prices for document delivery, you will most likely see an increase in the number of requests for the service. Because of the higher volume, you will be able to negotiate a better (lower) per unit price with your supplier.

A second option to lower prices is to align acquisitions with others, for instance, by working with other departments or even joining a consortium. By doing so, the volume of acquired units will go up, and therefore the price will go down. As you are negotiating as a group, your negotiation position will be much stronger as each member individually.

Increase the benefits

As discussed earlier in this chapter, customers need to be convinced of the benefits. If you increase the benefits, especially when compared with your competitors' benefits, your value will increase. Below are several ideas to increase the benefits.

Speed

If timely delivery of information is of value to your customers, decrease the turn-around time for delivering a research request or book order.

Personalisation

If you can target your service to a particular person instead of a generic service, the customer will see this as an increase in value. Think about how pleased Amazon.com users are with the recommendations of Amazon.com, a service which used to be standard in old-fashioned bookstores. Can you make your services become more personal, either by automation or by human interaction?

At your service

The most convincing benefit is excellent service. Do you know how your quality of service compares with that of your competitors? Especially when it comes to handling complaints or proactively solving problems, much can be won. If you deliver an excellent service, this will receive word of mouth promotion – something no marketing budget can buy.

Ease of use

You can also make your services easier to use. For instance, can your customers easily request services online via simple request forms? Can they use instant messaging to interact with the library? Is a summary included with each literature search report? Things like these will be seen as extra benefits of your services.

Reduce customers' costs

Last but not least, a component of enhancing your value is to help customers reduce their costs. Some ideas mentioned above already help them, but you can do more. Sit down with your customers and ask them how you can help them reduce their costs. Sometimes small changes on your side can help a customer in a big way. Not so long ago I met with an internal customer to discuss how the library could help them. One of their complaints was the cost of their departmental archive storage, which was very high as it was based on office space pricing. I explained we could store their archive much more cheaply off site, but still be able to retrieve items or boxes within a few hours. This not only reduced their departmental costs, but also resulted in a new library champion for us.

Using value-add as argument against outsourcing

Very often, libraries and information management activities are seen as 'cost centres' and not 'profit centres'. By increasing your value-added activities, you maximise your image of being a profit centre and minimise the image of being a cost centre.

When your management is considering outsourcing for your department or job, use the descriptions of your value-added services and products. You can combine these elements with other value-added elements like knowledge of organisational culture, confidentiality, business intimacy, flexibility and knowledge of the organisation's history.

The combination can be a successful case against a pure cost-reduction driven plan for outsourcing.

10

You have effective presentation skills

During your career as information professionals you will be faced with the challenge of giving a presentation, be it to your own small team or to an international audience at a conference. Over the years, I've spoken at many occasions to all kinds of audiences, but I still get mild stage fright when I have to get up and speak. At times like that, I think back to the job I had when I was at college: a tour guide. I was just 21 and very shy, the mere idea of talking in front of an audience, let alone entertaining them for two hours scared me witless. I realised that this fear would not help me in my career, so I really wanted to do something about it.

So I applied for the job of tour guide at the Dutch 'Office of the Future', which was a futuristic office designed by visionaries of information technology, office ergonomics, office design and environmental care. Visitors from different organisations would be given tours up to two hours long, where tour guides would show them around and discuss many topics. I had to learn the facts on almost 150 topics, many of them unknown to me at that time, but all essential to offer my guests a good tour.

I learned quickly, but my biggest fear was getting in front of a group and having their attention for over an hour. My mentor at that time was Remco de Haan, who taught me four valuable lessons:

- most people will already admire you for presenting;
- do not fear questions: in most cases you will know more than the audience and if you encounter a greater expert, learn from them;
- they will not bite – that's a promise;
- you will live through it and you will get better at it every time.

And after thousands of visitors, many presentations, and all kinds of mistakes, I became quite confident at giving presentations. Now, when I feel a little anxious I just think how far I have come since that very first presentation.

Tips and techniques

Have confidence

As mentioned previously, remember that most people will admire you just for presenting to an audience – they know how stressful it is. When you feel confident, your body language and speech will sound more trustworthy.

Know your audience

When your start thinking about your presentation, start gathering information on who your audience is, the size and what they are expecting. Are they a group of new recruits who need basic instructions on navigating the intranet, or are you presenting to a group of peers on a expert topic? If you are addressing a small group you know, you can be more interactive and informal compared with presenting to an audience of hundreds whom you have never met.

If you are invited to give a presentation to a group you do not know, find out about your audience in advance so you can tailor your presentation and maximise the chance of success.

Define the purpose of your presentation

Take time to define the purpose of your presentation, as this is the foundation for it: what do you want to achieve? Is it a single purpose, or do you have more objectives? Outline your purpose and test it with someone who can give feedback if the purpose is clear and concise. If you have more than one objective, define which one is the most important, what the order is, and how you will approach them.

Define your message

Once you have defined your purpose, you will need to define the message that you are going to send to your audience. Think of your presentation as a commercial: what message are you trying to convey? If you are giving a presentation on a new search engine, your message may be that the new search engine is powerful, yet easy to use. If you are presenting about an important reorganisation in your department, your message could be that we need to change in order to survive. That message should be very clear to your audience, as this is what you want them to take away from it.

Organise your presentation

You have now laid the foundation for your presentation, which you now need to put together. Work out how you want to take the audience towards the purpose of your presentation, and you will have a rough outline. Be aware of your time limit, however, as it is easy to try and squeeze too much into one presentation.

It is a good rule to introduce the objective(s) of your presentation, then talk about them, and at the end summarise what you have said. This maximises the chance that your message will reach the audience. Studies have shown that people often only remember less than half of the information right after the presentation, and that the percentage declines over time. Make the message stick by introducing it, telling it and recapping it.

Think of a storyline for your presentation which would make the most sense for the audience. The storyline can be different for every presentation, whether chronological, by process, by a list of tasks and results, or a list of problems and solutions.

Type of presentation

What type of presentation you will give depends on your message, your audience and your topic. The most common types of presentations are:

- *Discussion*: Usually the discussion is started with an introduction, then the presenter facilitates the discussion. At the end, the presenter summarises what has been discussed.

- *Demonstration*: You want to demonstrate a new way of working or introduce a new software application. Usually this is a combination of slides and then a 'live' demonstration of the application or work method. You can decide to go for a hands-on demonstration, where your audience gets to use new software or a piece of equipment.

- *Classroom or training*: This type of presentation is intended to enhance the audience's knowledge and is very interactive. For a large part, it focuses on explaining, relying on questions and answers. There is a fine line between a demonstration and training; often the training will start with a demonstration.

- *Speech or lecture*: The presenter talks to the audience with almost no interaction except for questions at the end.

The above shows the most generic types of presentations, but combinations are also possible.

Find support for your purpose

Gather input and material to support the purpose of your presentation. You may want to quote senior management's view on your topic, or influential external parties like a research firm or user survey. For example, if the purpose of your presentation is to convince your department about a new database, you may want to quote organisations that have implemented the database already and refer to your organisation's objective to work more efficiently in a standardised way.

Put your presentation to the test

Practise your presentation several times before your colleagues, your family or someone else who can give you feedback. It will ease your nerves and you will learn about the time it takes to deliver the presentation, things that are not clear to the audience and points of general improvement. Ask your test audience also to comment on your body language, as they will be able to give you an honest opinion.

Scout the setting

If possible, try to visit the setting where you will be presenting before your D-Day. Is it a large room with obstacles, so not every member of the audience has a clear view of you? Is it standing room only in an open office environment with all kinds of distraction? Knowing about the setting will greatly help you in envisioning how your presentation should be delivered and also prevents surprises on D-Day.

Prepare for the unexpected

We all know about Murphy's Law and have to be prepared for it. I once attended a presentation where the PowerPoint file that the presenter sent in was mixed up during the file transfer. Luckily, he had a CD-ROM with a backup – but Murphy struck again as the only PC in the room didn't have a CD-ROM drive. So prepare in advance for these manifestations of Murphy's Law – even think about how you will handle the presentation if there is no power: you could give hand-outs and deliver a presentation talking the audience through the presentation.

Unexpected things may also happen in the audience which may bring you off course. I once gave a presentation when a man in the last row of the audience suddenly fell through the floor. The floor of the presentation room was raised to allow the technicians to lay cables under it, and one tile had come loose causing that poor man to drop some 20 cm through the floor. He was not hurt, but I was completely off track. When such a thing happens, address the issue, make sure it is handled and get back on track. Briefly refer to what you were talking about before the unexpected event and pick up the storyline. Keep an eye on the time – you may have to skip or speed up certain parts to make up for the lost time.

There's no second chance for a first impression

Studies have shown that audiences will make up their minds about you within a few minutes, mainly based on how your look and how you sound. So look good – we make up our minds how we are going to react to someone before they speak. So, if you look and sound confident, people are more likely to give weight and value to what you are saying. Decide what you will wear – this also influences how your audience will perceive you.

In addition, remember to speak up and pace the tempo of your voice – we tend to increase our speed of talking when we are nervous. Reduce the speed of your voice until you think you are talking too slow, and that is usually just about right. Use the tone of your voice to emphasise certain words or concepts in your story; this is something you can practise when rehearsing your presentation.

The first act: your introduction

If you are introduced by a host or the previous speaker, make sure you meet with them before the presentation. Usually the host will ask you how you would like to be introduced, giving you the chance to give them some input. Often they will ask you for an anecdote linking your story to the general theme, making it easy for you to start your presentation.

If you are not introduced, you should introduce yourself by telling the audience who you are, why you are there, the purpose of the presentation and the outlay of the presentation. Mention how long your presentation will last and how you would like to handle questions: during or after the presentation.

Making and keeping contact with the audience

As I have already mentioned, body language makes up a large percentage of how the audience perceives you and receives your message. For this reason, making eye contact is essential. By looking at peoples' eyes we make clear contact, which is a very powerful technique during presentations. Make sure you make eye contact with the audience, for a few seconds per audience member – people will feel they are connected with you. If you have to look at your notes, alternate between looking at them and keeping eye contact with the audience.

Another way of keeping contact with the audience is moving on the stage or even moving close to the audience. Our eyes are naturally trained to follow moving objects, so your audience will pay more attention if you move. Check the stage or area before your presentation to see how much space you have to move around.

Finally, involve the audience by asking them questions. They can answer by raising their hands or perhaps you can ask a member of the audience directly. This is a change of scenery for the audience and is often a welcome variation of purely listening to a speaker.

Emphasise your presentation using gestures

Besides varying the tone of your voice, you can emphasise certain parts of your presentation by using gestures. You can use three different types of gestures:

- *conventional gestures* to give visual dimension to your words (e.g. holding up your hand to visualise 'stop' or pointing at the audience to emphasise 'you');
- *descriptive gestures* to represent an idea (e.g. using your hands to indicate something which is large or small, round or square); and
- *emotional gestures* to communicate feelings (e.g. pounding the lectern in anger).

These gestures should only be used if they fit with how you act naturally, otherwise they will seem over-the-top. During your rehearsals, check with your test audience how your gestures are perceived.

Once, twice, three times your message

We have all learned this very basic but vital rule: tell people what you are going to tell them, tell them and end by telling them what you have told including what you want them to do following your presentation.

Repeating your message is key to making it stick. Watch carefully how professional presenters or politicians constantly weave their message in their presentation, making sure their message is received.

Do not read your slides word for word

For me, the most annoying presentations are the ones where the presenter literally reads all the words on the slide. Audiences can read your slides, so do not repeat what is up there. Put as few words on the slides as possible, so the audience can focus on you speaking. If it is very important the audience reads a certain sentence or paragraph on a slide, tell them you will pause to allow them to read it. Most people can only process information via one sense at a time: if they are reading, they cannot listen.

Don't get sidetracked by disruptions

If your presentation is disrupted, do not get sidetracked for too long. When a cell phone rings, the public address system makes weird noises or an unexpected sound is heard, if at all possible, ignore the disruption. If you cannot ignore it, address it, and if necessary ask your host to handle it.

Get back to your presentation by recapping briefly what you told before the disruption. Stick to your agenda and try to recoup the lost time by leaving out or shortening some parts of your presentation.

Watch the clock

As you have practised, you know how long your presentation will last. Stick to this length as this will be greatly appreciated by the audience and other speakers. People will like you for using less time or catching up for the extra time other speakers used. I often ask the host to warn me with a hand signal when I am halfway during my allotted time and five minutes before the end. This way it is easier to focus on the presentation and not be preoccupied by the clock.

Wrap up

The ending of your presentation should be the message that you want people to leave with and what you want them to do. Reinforce that message and make it seem a logical end to your presentation.

Thank the audience for their attention and if that was the plan, invite them for questions and answers. You may want to give the audience some time to think of a question and actually ask the question. If there are no immediate questions from the audience, you can use questions to solicit questions – ask open-ended questions related to the topic. For example, you could ask 'After my presentation, do you feel more comfortable using product X or using process Y?'

When a member of the audience wants to start a discussion, do not let this take up too much time. Suggest that you will discuss the issue with them after the presentation or promise a follow-up to their comments. Do not immediately judge their comments, but mention that others may have questions as well that should be addressed.

Ultimately, even though many of us will never really enjoy making presentations, the techniques mentioned above and lots of practice will surely help you survive them.

11

You know how to measure value

Once you have created and enhanced value-added services and products, there will come a time that you have to prove you have done so. Value is intangible, but you will have to measure it.

Several years ago my company went through a drastic reorganisation, which could have resulted in major budget cuts for many of the services departments. My department was part of a mid-sized unit, which had always valued information management services. The unit manager had always given us more priority regarding budget and staffing compared with the headquarters' general policy, as he was convinced that we were essential for the future of his unit.

So our department had to justify our management's extra investments by proving that every dollar spent had resulted in more value. We were fortunate to have the help of several managers, who had dealt with such challenges before.

Over the course of a few weeks, we built a business case for our department by gathering different statements of our value. Our first line of defence was a total overview of our costs compared with our budget recovery percentage. Second were examples where customers stated how much time and money we saved them by providing services like proper records management and literature searching.

We used these examples to provide estimates on how much value we had generated over the years. For example, if we save one hour per week per employee by keeping the project files up to date, and the average hourly fee per employee is x dollars, we have saved the company x times the number of employees minus the costs for the file clerk.

Finally, we summarised the outcome of our annual customer survey, which clearly indicated we were customer driven and that our services were seen as indispensable.

When our unit manager had to discuss the reorganisation plans with his manager at the headquarters, he was complimented on the report we had created. They even wanted to develop our report on value measurement into a best practice for all services departments.

Best practice for measuring value

This chapter prepares you for the challenge of measuring value by presenting practical tips and experiences.

Claim your value

As it is by nature hard to calculate your department's value added, as most of your value is intangible, the easiest strategy is to simply claim your value. You can claim this by using internal relationships, knowledge of influential stakeholders and word-of-mouth to establish that your department contributes value. Make your claim believable with a few proven examples where your department clearly proved its worth and repeat them.

The numbers game

Instead of trying to calculate the return on investment (ROI) or a full report on value measures, dazzle management with statistics from your department. Show them the volume of information requests you handle, how fast they are answered, the volume of articles you order, the number of visitors to your website etc. As with the previous tip about claiming your value, this is more about politics and creating an image, but very often it works.

The 'more official' numbers game

If you want to set up a structured set of value measures, think about input/output measures and efficiency measures.

Input/output measures are about collecting data on topics you can quantify, such as your budget, how the budget is spent, the number of items catalogued, number of loans, and user satisfaction. You can measure user satisfaction in several ways, which I will describe in more detail later in this chapter.

The efficiency measures are the time and costs of each activity in your department. You create a grouped list of all the activities in your department and then you calculate how much time and costs are related to each item. This gives management an insight on how productive your department is, although it only measures quantity and not quality.

User satisfaction survey

As Sebastian Mundt described in his paper on user satisfaction:

All efforts put into satisfying library customers are based on the insight that services are not primarily chosen for their objective properties but first of all for their perceived fitness for purpose in the customers' eyes. Satisfaction surveys are an established means to collect and gather these subjective judgments of single customers and convert them into a complex, objectified 'snapshot'. (Mundt, 2003)

User satisfaction surveys are very useful to demonstrate your value to your management and the rest of the organisation. However, they have to be set up properly and require a concentrated effort. I will describe a short summary of the steps:

- *How will you measure satisfaction?* As the dictionary explains, satisfaction is the fulfilment of a need or want. Study what satisfaction means to your users and how you could describe it.

- *How will you gather the data for the survey?* Some data you can retrieve via your systems, such as the number of website visitors or the number of requests. Other data can be gathered in a variety of ways to survey your users, for instance, via a paper questionnaire, a web/intranet survey or focused user panels.

- *Gather the data.* This is the actual activity where you collect the data for your satisfaction survey, from one or more sources.

- *Analyse the data.* When you have gathered all the data, you can analyse it in relation to the satisfaction measurements you have decided upon.

- *Recommend and implement improvements.* Based on the outcome of the satisfaction survey, you can see the points of improvement for your department.

- *Repeat.* A user satisfaction survey is just a snapshot and should be repeated to measure improvements.

There is more to user satisfaction surveys than I can describe in a few paragraphs, so do read a proper book or follow a course to prepare yourself for such a project.

Narratives and anecdotal evidence

Besides hard numbers and a more qualitative perspective based on user satisfaction, another powerful addition to your value statement is collecting narratives and anecdotal evidence. In combination with quantitative and qualitative measures, you can use narratives from key customers to complete your value statement. You can use a quote from one or more key users on your department's value to them or even include a short interview. Such a story can appeal to management as it shows that customers have not only perceived your value, but also want to testify it.

Return on investment

ROI is seen by management as an important, objective and accurate measure of value. The acronym refers to the percentage of profit or revenue generated from a specific activity. The ROI data proves whether your department's services and products have produced cost savings and if they have resulted in revenue.

As a services department, however, is it not easy to calculate the ROI as much of your value is not directly visible in cost savings or revenues. If you are looking for cost savings, think about centralising purchasing (including discount possibilities), merging smaller contracts into corporate wide contracts, cancelling little-used subscriptions and cutting your hardcopy collection to save on office space.

Finding out if and how your department's activities have resulted in revenue can only be gathered from users. Below are a few examples:

- *Have they saved time by using your services?* This can be translated into a dollar value by multiplying the time saved by the average hourly wage or fee.

- *Do customers have examples where your department helped them to generate revenue?* If you work with sales staff, your information may have been crucial in creating the perfect sales presentation. In another area you may have prevented problems with a new supplier by providing management with an overview of that supplier's financial details and news profile.

- *Did you save the organisation money in legal costs?* These days, providing the right information in relation to a legal cause can save an organisation huge amounts of money and time.

Calculating the ROI is the ratio of savings and revenue, divided by the cost of your department, which you multiply by 100 to express as a percentage. The ROI is always calculated over a predefined period, often a year. If the percentage is above a 100 per cent, you have delivered ROI.

It will be clear that calculating ROI is a complicated exercise. Therefore, you could decide not to calculate the ROI for the whole department but for specific services or projects.

ROV instead of ROI

Where ROI is a very 'hard' measure, ROV (return on value) takes soft benefits into account. These are benefits that are seen as desirable, but are difficult to quantify using financial metrics. The ROV complements the ROI analysis by including both the financial costs and hard returns, and also the intangible benefits. Examples of more intangible benefits are more information literate employees, more satisfied employees and a knowledge sharing culture.

ROV is not easy to calculate, as it looks at more components than ROI and also requires you to put a dollar value on intangible benefits. As an organisation these are hard questions, but are certainly very relevant when considering the value of a department. If you are interested in ROV, please enlist the help of an expert.

Balanced scorecard

Another approach for measuring value is the balanced scorecard. Kaplan and Norton (1992) proposed this methodology in an article published in the *Harvard Business Review*. It describes a method to link an organisation's strategic and financial goals. It combines different components of a business into one report: the balanced scorecard. Management uses the balanced scorecard like a pilot relies on the dials and indicators in the cockpit of an aeroplane. They need detailed information on a number of aspects of the flight, but relying on a single instrument could give a wrong impression of the status. Based on this example, the performance of one part of the business will inevitably have an impact on other areas.

The balanced scorecard uses four perspectives to look at a business:

- *The customer perspective*: This is how your customers see your department, measuring service quality, performance and cost.

- *The internal perspective*: This represents the goals that relate to core competencies, skills, quality, and cost measures.

- *The innovation and learning perspective*: This relates to your department's new services, service and product improvements and skills. For example, qualifications (like ISO 9002) your department has achieved and courses taken by staff to enhance or broaden their skill set.

- *The financial perspective*: Financial performance measures of your department can include cash flow, market share, return on capital investments and volume of growth as compared with the industry norm.

The balanced scorecard looks at a broad spectrum of elements to measure the value, but like measuring ROI, this is not something done easily. A very useful taxonomy of information services value elements was developed by Kantor and Saracevic (1997). A selection of this taxonomy could be used by departments to build a balanced scorecard for their purpose.

External reports

In combination with other measurements, you can also quote published literature on the value of information and information services. If you are a member of a library association or another information professional association, they will often have a bibliography on this topic. Management will be especially interested in this information if you can quote dollar values from peers in your industry.

Benchmarking

An interesting way to show your department's value is to benchmark against other information services departments and demonstrate your position. Not only will you learn how you compare with your peers, but you can also learn from those who do better on certain topics.

The end result of a benchmarking exercise is not just a report of how you compare, but what you will improve and how based on the benchmark.

Although benchmarking requires a fair amount of work, it will help you prove your department's value and gain professional relationships with peers. If you want to improve your processes and services continuously, having a close relationship with peers is especially valuable.

The benchmarking process consists of six steps:

- *Describe why and what you want to benchmark*: 'Why' you want to benchmark should be described to make the goals clear to all involved. Second, make clear what services and/or processes you will benchmark. You will have to define them for this study to provide clarity to your benchmarking partners.

- *Develop measures*: It is essential to develop measures for each element that you want to benchmark. Each measure should be definable and realistic to obtain. For example, will you measure staff by headcount or full-time equivalent?

- *Find benchmarking partners*: Now you need to find partners that you want to benchmark against. You will want to look for partners that either are in the same industry or are otherwise comparable. Benchmarking partners can be found via your personal network, a professional association or by references.

- *Collect and analyse data*: Once you have a benchmarking agreement and sometimes a confidentiality agreement with your partners, start the study. When you have collected all the data, you can start analysis – how does each partner rank?

- *Recommend improvements*: If one or more partners outrank your department, ask to interview the highest performers. They will have 'best practices' which you can adopt to improve your efficiency and effectiveness.

- *Present to stakeholders and management*: Now you are ready to present the benchmarking outcome to your management and other stakeholders, such as your customer panel and department staff.

12

You manage your time and use the magical word 'no'

Deep down, the main reason for me to be in the information profession is the need to help others. Every time I am able to help someone, I feel good. Whether it is an answer to a quick reference question that helps someone on the phone, or a multimillion dollar search engine project where I am responsible for meeting the user's search requirements: I am in it because of my desire to help others.

This driver, however, has a downside: I find it hard to say 'no' to a request. Over the years I have learned that I need to learn how to manage my time and say 'no' in order to reach my goals. I still find it hard at first when I cannot commit to someone's request, but I am getting better at doing the right things for the right reasons.

Setting priorities and keeping to schedule

All time-management books and courses have priority setting as one of the key themes. In order to make the most of your available time and energy, you will have to focus on what is a priority and what not. When you define your priorities, you need to balance between personal values and organisational values. Before you begin to set priorities in your business and personal life, be clear about your values. In order to achieve effectiveness, your personal values should be in line with what you do. If they are not in line, you will feel dissatisfied and unhappy – leading to reduced effectiveness and long-term frustration.

When you have defined your values, gather information on the values and priorities of the organisation where you work. A good start will be your manager or mentor, who can give you an insight into your organisation's strategy and business plan. You should be able to fit your projects and tasks to these higher-level plans and derive the priorities. Your priorities should be linked to your organisation's priorities. Make it a habit to find that link: how can you link your work to your organisation's priorities using only a few sentences.

When it comes to setting priorities on a lower level, a good method is the A-B-C-D-E method, which you can use on a daily or weekly basis. For each task you assign one of the letters, indicating the priority of that particular task.

A stands for a 'must do'. If you do not do this, it will have serious negative consequences. If you have more than one 'A' task, organise them by importance using numbers like A-1, A-2, A-3, etc. When you begin work, start with A-1 as this is your top priority.

B stands for 'should do' but less important than an 'A' task. Not completing a B task will have minor negative consequences.

C stands for 'nice to do'; but ranks below 'A' and 'B'. C tasks have no negative consequences for not completing.

D stands for 'delegate', as this is the type of task that others can do as well or even better. This frees up more time for the most important tasks that only you can do.

E stands for 'eliminate'. These are the tasks that you can stop doing without any effect, as they have little or no value.

When you use the A-B-C-D-E method, you create a good overview of what is important and unimportant. When followed regularly, this will focus your time and energy on those items on your list that that determine your success or failure.

Should you be doing something?

Your time is always limited, so you need to do the right things in the right way. Being effective is about doing the right things. This is related to the priority setting of time management, discussed earlier. I find it very useful to ask myself the questions 'Does *this* have to be done?' and then 'Should *I* be doing this?' Consider whether a task, a chore or a project really needs to be done: how does this tie to your priorities? Do not fear having this discussion with your colleagues, customer or manager. Often, when you can explain why a task is not that important in your opinion, the other can be convinced to share your view. For example, your boss wants you to brief him personally every week on the detailed status of all your projects and tasks. If you can explain to him that this will take valuable time away from priorities, but that you will brief him on the most important projects and tasks, he may find this acceptable. Think about this before accepting any new tasks.

Second, are you the right person to be doing it? Something may be very important, but you are not always the right person for it. If it does not fit your scope of work, your skills or time schedule it is better to have someone else to do it. Revisit these two reasons for yourself and with your team regularly.

Saying 'no'

This is one of the most difficult things to do, especially for most information professionals whose key motto is 'customer service' and who want to be nice to everyone. But as our time is limited, we have to learn how to turn down requests for our attention and time if needed.

If you have your list of priorities, and they are agreed with your management – stick to them. As many other people, you will be tempted to take on more work when being asked. Being service minded, your first reaction may be to accept it, or you find it hard to say 'no' to a request. Saying 'no' gets easier when you know what you should do (things to which you will say 'yes') and which things are not on your priority list ('no'). This makes explaining your 'no' easier to the requestor.

There is a variety of ways of saying 'no'. First of all, try to avoid being the one that has to say 'no'. If someone asks you to do something that is not on your priorities list, but you find it hard to decline a request, you can use your manager. Reply to the requestor that you would like to help them, but as it is not on your list of priorities as agreed with your manager, and that they should discuss this with your manager first.

Another polite way of declining a request is to ask if you can answer the next day. This extra time allows you to think about the commitment you will be making before making a quick decision. And when you have doubts about a request, that is a sure sign to decline. Be honest with the requestor, let them know of your doubts or why you are saying 'no'. Tell them you appreciate them asking you, but that you cannot give this request the commitment it requires.

Finally, you can propose a compromise instead of saying flat-out 'no'. If you cannot do precisely what the requestor wants, perhaps you can find a different solution that is satisfactory. For example, if someone needs a large literature search done by tomorrow, describe what you could get accomplished by tomorrow. If that is not satisfactory, describe what you could deliver in two days or a week until you reach a compromise that is satisfactory for both.

Remember that if you do not use the word 'no', you will only increase your workload and your level of stress – which ultimately does not help you, your colleagues or your customers.

Keep a 'to do' list

In order for me to feel on top of things, I always keep my PDA at hand with my 'to do' list. If something pops into my mind, or I am being asked to do something, I put it on my 'to do' list. This releases me from having to remember everything, and gives me an overview of everything I should do. During the day, I review my 'to do' list and review which tasks I should discuss with other people in order to delegate them. Then I look at my tasks and plan them in my calendar.

Be efficient

Focus first on effectiveness (knowing the right things to do), and second on efficiency (doing it right). In essence, being efficient comes down to doing things in a minimum amount of time. A good way of becoming more efficient is to take a detailed look at your day. Keep a time log for a week and note what you are doing and when. After a week, you will know where your time goes and you can start rearranging your work. For example:

- if you have to make lots of phone calls, try to cluster them on certain days or at certain times;
- the same goes for other tasks you can cluster, e.g. the time writing, or processing bills;

- don't be tempted by the 'you have new mail' sound – block time in your calendar for reading and responding to e-mails;

- do not fill your calendar to the max, allow time for interruptions and distractions – a good rule of the thumb is to fill 50 per cent of your time upfront;

- block time to prepare for meetings and presentations, instead of showing up without knowing what the meeting is about – which would be a waste of time;

- learn from the best – if you know someone who is really efficient, ask if they can share some tips, often they will be very willing to teach you how they do things efficiently.

Remember that it is not just enough to be efficient, you also have to be effective – or you will be doing the wrong things efficiently.

Hidden time

If you have kept a time log, you will also find 'hidden time': time that you did not know you could use. For example, I commute by train almost three hours per day. This gives me a good amount of time to catch up on reading articles and thinking about my work. I find it hard to find suitable time at work to do this, and so I am now using my commute time useful. You can use other hidden time in the gym (you can listen to podcasts or spoken books), waiting in airports or the time waiting for the helpdesk when your computer is broken.

Delegating

Delegating is very useful, but only when done properly – otherwise you may not get what you want or spend more time re-doing it. Describe what you want to delegate and find the right person for this task or project. Make sure that you explain what should be done by the person you are delegating to, as they may not be aware of everything you know. Agree the milestones with the delegate, as well as when you will expect progress updates and in which cases you need to be informed (e.g. an emergency or budget overspend). For the delegate it is very important that you trust them to do it right. Nothing is more frustrating than being delegated a task, and then constantly being watched or corrected while doing it.

Delegate upwards

If your manager can delegate downwards, you also have the choice to delegate upwards! You should only do this if you feel the relationship with your manager allows this, and it should be used sparsely. Say, for example, you have been appointed as a project leader for an ambitious cross-department project, but the other departments fail to attend your meetings or meet your deadlines. For a while you have been chasing project participants and trying to get the project on track, but it is in danger of derailing. By involving your manager in this problem, they might be able to use their status to get the other departments into action.

Got a minute?

Be warned when someone asks you 'have you got a minute?' That hardly ever means that it will take only one minute – usually a lengthy discussion will take place interrupting your work. When confronted with this question, make it a habit to ask 'Can you tell me briefly what is it about?' Listen to the explanation and decide whether you should handle this right now or that you should schedule something. If you think it is something that needs a scheduled discussion, you can answer by telling the requestor that you agree it is important, but that you need to check a document or talk to a colleague. Then agree on a time and date for the discussion.

Know thyself

We all know how our body rhythm works, i.e. when we are at our best regarding concentration and energy. Plan your day and week according to the highs and lows of your body rhythm, making the best of your time and energy.

Starter, doer or finisher?

The type of worker you are also plays a role in time management. There are many different studies and books on this topic, but I'd like to highlight three broad types of worker here that may influence how you manage your time: the starter, the doer and the finisher. If you are a starter, you like to invent and start new things, but once the novelty wears off, you find it hard to be motivated. A doer (also known as the company worker) has pride in doing things efficiently, as long as they know what needs to be done and how. If you are a doer, you find it hard to get started on new things as you do not know exactly what to do and how. The last type of worker is the finisher, who likes to see things through to the end and making sure everything is done. The finisher does not like uncertainties and often gets caught up in the details.

You surely recognise which type of worker you are, so you know your strengths and weaknesses. You will also recognise your friends and colleagues in these types, so consult them if needed. If you are a starter, and you find it hard to finish tasks or projects, look around in your network for someone who is a finisher – they will surely be able to tell you how they would deal with it.

Rewards

Remember when you were a kid, and your mother promised you an ice cream if you did your homework assignment well? Or how your father gave you extra pocket money when you helped him clean out the attic? Even as adults, we like rewards, and the normal pay cheque is not always the sufficient award to motivate. So reward yourself, especially for work you are not too fond of. For example, I do not typically enjoy writing project management documents. However, in my company no project can be done without terms of reference, a business plan or a project plan. So whenever I have to create such a document, I promise myself I will treat myself to a tasty snack or delicious dessert when it is finished.

Deadlines

As my favourite author Douglas Adams once stated: 'I love deadlines. I like the whooshing sound they make as they fly by.' Most of us do not like deadlines, but we have to live with them.

If you have a deadline imposed on you, verify whether it is feasible to meet that deadline considering the effort required, your other workload and dependencies on others (e.g. approval from the marketing department who only meet once a month). When you know a deadline is not feasible, do engage with the colleague or manager who is imposing the deadline. If you know upfront that you cannot meet the deadline, it will not only be a burden to you, but it is also a risk for the project or task. The least you will get out of this discussion is that you brought it up but the deadline does not change. In some cases, the other will agree with your arguments (which they may not have known about) and the deadline may be changed or you will get extra resources.

Keep this in mind when you are setting deadlines: nobody works in a vacuum, so people's capability of meeting deadlines also depends on resources and decisions which you are not (yet) aware of.

Tackle distractions

During your day, little and big distractions keep you away from being productive. A colleague may drop in unannounced for a long and trivial discussion, the phone will ring at all times or the sound of the fax machine around the corner may be distracting you. Agree with your co-workers what the sign is when you do not want to be disturbed, such as closing your door or a sign on your desk. If it is possible in your job, create blocks of 'phone time' during your day during which you will listen to voicemail and return phone calls. Communicate those times to those who call you, so they know when they can reach you directly. When noises distract you, try to find if you can do something about them: send in a complaint about that noisy fax machine, wear headphones with classical music or perhaps you can move to a quieter spot when you need to concentrate.

13

You know the basics of information architecture

Ever since I joined the industry, I find it hard to know what job title to use to reflect what I do. Having worked in commercial organisations, there has been a tendency for management to change my job title regularly, so over the years I have been 'information specialist', 'knowledge steward' and 'cybrarian'. But these titles never captured precisely what I was looking for.

As my area of interest has always been the cross-section between content, technology and users, I have always looked for a job title that reflects this. A few years ago I read an article on 'information architecture', and I thought this was a very good description of my work and interest.

In my opinion, information architecture is a natural extension of what librarians have done for many years. It opens new career opportunities for information professionals and increases our visibility in the future. I would encourage you to not just to read this chapter on information architecture, but also to think how you and your team fit into this growing area. Information architects will be key jobs for organisations and our society for the future – and information professionals should be key players in shaping this exciting new profession.

Definitions

According to the Wikipedia:

> ...the term information architecture describes a specialised skill set which relates to the management of information and employment of information related tools. It also has some degree of association with library sciences due to the nature of information relationships and management of information content. Many library schools teach information architecture as a part of their curriculum.[1]

This definition already contains the clear link to library science, as this is one of the important roots for information architecture.

One of the pioneers in information architecture is Louis Rosenfeld, who, with Peter Morville, wrote the original information architecture bible *Information Architecture for the World Wide Web*. This defines information architecture as: 'the process of structuring and organising information so that it is easier for users to find and for owners to maintain'. The shortest, but perhaps best summary of information architecture is:

context + content = information architecture

Any librarian or information professional will be able to relate to this definition, as this is at the core of what we are about: putting content (be it books or bits) into context (be it a shelving scheme or web taxonomy).

I would argue that information professionals have understood this far better than all others involved in information management – but we should expand our skills to become all-round information architects. More on this later in this chapter.

The need for information architects started in the mid-1990s, when we noticed an unprecedented growth in information networks, such as online databases, intranets and of course the Internet. Most often websites were poorly structured, and there was rarely a blueprint for the management of content or user navigation.

Hence, the pitfall of information overload – one of the original goals of building databases, intranets and websites – has not been avoided.

Outside of organisations, we have seen a similar trend in our society where we have to cope with more information every day and rely on more information. More people than ever have access to a vast amount of information. According to the 'How much information is there?' report (UC Berkeley's School of Information Management and Systems, 2003), almost 800 MB of recorded information is produced per person each year, the majority of which is stored on magnetic media. To illustrate how much new information this represents, the report describes that it would take about 30 feet of books to store this amount of information on paper.

The main problem with this information explosion is whether we can find the information we need in information systems and use it?

As architects define plans for buildings that have a purpose now and many years in the future, be it a house, an office or a townhouse, information architects should define how information systems should be built and used.

Information architects

So what exactly is the job of an information architect? Richard Saul Wurman defined information architects quite clearly in his book *Information Architects*:

Information Architect:

1. the individual who organises the patterns inherent in data, making the complex clear;
2. a person who creates the structure or map of information, which allows others to find their personal paths to knowledge;
3. the emerging twenty-first century professional occupation addressing the needs of the age focused on clarity, human understanding, and the science of the organisation of information. (Wurman, 1996)

The definition shows that an information architect is a multidisciplinary job, relying on different disciplines to become an all-round professional. If we compare the definition above to more traditional library science job descriptions, we can see interesting parallels.

Both information architects and information professionals focus on helping others to find information by designing structures to guide them. Where the more traditional library discipline is rooted in the paper-based information society, information architecture was established during the web society. So where 'traditional' information professionals were trained to work with catalogues and thesauri, information architects use website design and taxonomies. But in essence, the principles both apply to solve a similar problem.

Mike Steckel likened Ranganathan's legendary five laws of library science to the field of information architecture, applied to website design as a modern example:

1. Books are for use.

   Websites are designed to be used, they are not temples or statues we admire from a distance. We want people to interact with our websites, click around, do things, and have fun.

2. Every book its reader.

3. Every reader its book.

   Maybe we can modify these two to say 'each piece of content its user' and 'each user his/her content'. The point here is that we should add content with specific user needs in mind, and we should make sure that readers can find the content they need. Laws 2 and 3 remind me of the methodology taught by Adaptive Path. Make certain our content is something our users have identified as a need, and at the same time make sure we don't clutter up our site with content no one seems to care about.

4. Save the time of the user.

   This law, when we are talking of websites, has both a front-end component (make sure people quickly find what they are looking for) and a back-end component (make sure our data is structured in a way that retrieval can be done quickly). It is also imperative that we understand what goals our users are trying to achieve on our site.

5. The library is a living organism.

   We need to plan and build with the expectation that our sites and our users will grow and change over time. Similarly we need to always keep our own skill levels moving forward. (Steckel, 2002)

As shown above, the information architecture discipline could be a natural new path for information professionals. With a deepened understanding of the other disciplines involved in information architecture like usability design, communication, architecture, visual design, and information technology the information professional is an ideal candidate for this role.

Key information architecture skills

In an organisation, the information architect is the intermediary between several groups to solve information management challenges: end users, web designers, search engine developers and management. Each of these wants something from the information architect, and the information architect requires something from each of them to finish the project successfully.

As an information architect you need to be a jack-of-all-trades and should be able to communicate with each of these groups on an acceptable level. You will need to explain soft end user requirements to IT developers. For example, an end user requirement may be: 'I want to find the information most relevant to my job without looking for it all over on the intranet', which is too vague for an IT developer. By using interviewing skills and knowledge of what technically is possible using web design, search engines and other IT features, the information architect should be able to bridge this gap between developers and end users.

As another example, I was once asked to design an overarching navigation design for a global intranet. This would cover hundreds of websites, many different topics and should be easy to understand from a top level for end users but also allow flexibility for growth in the future. In order to come up with a design, I spoke extensively with different end users how they found intranet websites and what their intuitive take was on a navigation design. Of course, at first I got as many different takes as the number of users I spoke to, but later on I was able to distinguish these views into broader categories:

- location (e.g. the country homepages of different companies);
- discipline (e.g. accountancy, tax, and consultancy);

- service (e.g. financial audit, IT security consultancy, enterprise resource planning consultancy);
- keywords/topics (e.g. project names, 'hot topics' all sorted alphabetically).

During the design of the top level navigation design I used different skills:

- *user interviewing*: extracting the information I needed from users;
- *logical thinking*: purely logical reasoning what should be logical for users to understand;
- *structuring information*: finding the common categories in all the data I had gathered from the end users;
- *basic understanding of web design*: a website should be simple and not be confusing, so the navigation design should be to the point.

In order to broaden your information architecture skills, work with others who have the skills you would like to acquire.

I have learned a lot about website design by working on several intranets with a number of skilled web designers. Their experience, especially in what will and will not work with end users, has helped me a lot. As a librarian, I am used to reading text on a screen and figuring out what to do, but from the web designers I have learned that well selected icons or pictures are better suited for end users. Pictures are easier to recognise and prettier to look at than words, so using a picture of a magnifying glass for 'search' on an website is often better than just putting 'click here for search' on the screen.

If you are interested in information architecture, there is a vast collection of articles, presentations and discussions available. A good collection is the website of The Asilomar Institute for Information Architecture. This is a non-profit international volunteer organisation dedicated to advancing and promoting information architecture. Check out their library of resources on information architecture at *http://iainstitute.org/*.

So do not be intimidated by information architecture, as you may already be more of an information architect than you realise.

Notes

1. *http://en.wikipedia.org/wiki/Information_architecture.*
2. For more information on Ranganathan's laws, see: *en.wikipedia.org/wiki/S._R._Ranganathan.*

14

You speak the technical jargon

Information technology has changed our profession and has provided us with new visions and solutions. As with any other discipline, IT has its own jargon full of buzzwords and acronyms. In order to understand most of what is relevant for an information professional, I have compiled a glossary in this chapter.

A glossary of terms

This is not meant as a complete dictionary, but these words are essential to understand current IT trends and topics relevant for you. After reading this chapter you can at least get a gist of what your IT colleagues are talking about and can explain *in their words* what you need from technology. The glossary will also help you to gain a better understanding of the different concepts and technologies in the field of information and library science.

As IT is changing, you can use this chapter as a foundation to learn more. There are many different IT dictionaries on the Web, alternatively, you can use Google to find other definitions of words – just type 'define <word>' to query different glossaries and dictionaries.

Application programming interface (API)

This is the interface between the operating system and application programs. It defines how applications communicate with the operating system and other applications.

For example, your library catalogue may have an API which allows a search engine to interact with the library catalogue. Another example is the Google web API for developers which enables them to easily find and manipulate information from the Google indexes.

Architecture

Just like a house, the architecture (often used in the context of IT) refers to the way different components fit and work together. Within IT there are different sets of architecture, such as software architecture, which describes how applications interact, and network architecture, related to the different components of a network and their interaction. See also *information architecture.*

ASCII

Pronounced 'askee', this is the acronym for American Standard Code for Information Interchange, as defined by the American National Standards Institute (ANSI). This defines a file format standard to achieve compatibility between different applications and hardware. The ASCII set consists of 128 characters, including letters, numbers, punctuation, and control codes.

Authentication

The authentication determines the identity of a user and what they are allowed to access. Most used forms of IT authentication are smartcards, passwords, digital signatures and Internet Protocol (IP) addresses. For example, a website may provide access to its archives for a certain group of users based on their range of IP addresses. See also *IP number.*

Bitmap

An image represented as pixels ('dots') in a row and column format.

Boolean search

Boolean is a set of search operators to include or exclude certain words.

- Using the 'AND' operator between terms retrieves documents containing both terms: 'dog AND cat' will retrieve only documents containing both the word 'dog' and 'cat'.
- The 'OR' operator retrieves documents containing either term: 'dog OR cat' will retrieve documents with the words 'dog' or 'cat'.
- Finally, 'NOT' excludes the retrieval of term(s) from your search: dog NOT cat will retrieve the documents that contain the word 'dog', but exclude the documents with the word 'cat'.

Bug

When software or hardware contains a fault or flaw, this is referred to as a bug. The term has its roots in a malfunction in one of the very first modern computers, the Mark I in 1945. The computer malfunctioned because a moth was contained between the circuits of the long glass-enclosed computer. From that moment on, problems with computers were referred to as bugs.

Cache

A place in a computer's memory (RAM) or on storage medium (hard disk) to hold recently accessed data, designed to speed up further access to the same set of data. For example, a web browser cache stores the pages, graphics, and URLs of website you have visited in a cache file on your hard drive. When you return to that website, it will retrieve the website from the cache, so that everything does not have to be downloaded again.

Cascading style sheets (CSS)

Cascading style sheets are definitions that describe how a document should be presented on the Web using style templates. These templates are stored separately from the web page itself and provide more control over fonts, colours, headers, borders, etc. By using CSS, the content (the web page itself) is separated from the design (the CSS file) as opposed to HTML files where content and design are mixed.

CGI script

A computer program that uses the common gateway interface (CGI) standard to run a program or script from a web server. When a user clicks on a link to a CGI script, the program or script on the web server is run and the results are returned to the browser. For example, a CGI script can be used to execute a query on a database and return the results to a web page.

Client/server

A type of so-called distributed system (see *distributed computing*) in which software has been split between a server and a client. Most often, the server is a powerful central computer and a client is a standard PC from a user. The client sends requests to a server asking for information or action to which the server responds. Large accounting systems often operate using the client/software model: the local user PC only contains the user interface, which interacts with the central server for data retrieval, complex computations and reporting.

Compatible

When software or hardware is compatible, it means it can interact with other hardware or software without problems. In the last century, most computers were labelled as MS-DOS compatible, meaning they could run the MS-DOS operating system without any problems.

Compression

A method of removing redundant and or non-critical data in digital files to reduce the file size. This saves disk space and reduces the bandwidth needed to transfer the file.

Concept search

Instead of searching on words itself, a concept search searches on the semantic meaning of words. For example, when searching on the word 'company', the concept search will expand to also include related words like 'business' or 'organisation'.

Cookie

A cookie is a very small data file created on your own computer when you access certain websites, usually to store your preferences or settings. When you return to that particular website, the website will retrieve the cookie and 'recognise' you.

Database

A database is a structured collection of data records that can be accessed electronically. A record is the equivalent of a paper index card, containing the same set of attributes.

Database management system (DBMS)

The DBMS is a set of programs to organise, verify, store and retrieve data from the database. Well-known DBMS are Oracle, Microsoft Access or Microsoft SQL Server.

Distributed computing

This refers to the use of multiple computers collaborating via a network to achieve a single task.

Domain name system (DNS)

The DNS translates domain names (like *www.dennie .heye.nl*) into the unique Internet Protocol (IP) numbers (213.206.89.190) to find the correct website. The DNS is a hierarchy of domains, subdomains, sites, and hosts.

Dublin Core

This is a standard, minimal set of elements (title, creator, date, etc.) with optional qualifiers to describe digital information objects, much like a library catalogue. The use of Dublin Core is encouraged to achieve exchange of metadata and better indexing by search engines.

Encryption

The process of scrambling a message so that a key, held only by authorised recipients, is needed to unscramble and read the message. Encryption is mostly used to transfer for data over a public network or safe storage on a medium.

Extranet

The extranet refers to a part of the intranet that is open to an authorised third party, be it customers, staff or partners. The intranet is safely guarded from the Internet by a firewall, whereas the extranet part is accessible via the Internet with authentication.

Federated search

If you have a collection of different information sources (websites or databases), each with their own search engine, a federated search can be used to use one 'umbrella' search engine to cover all of them. The federated search engine sends the query to all the connected information sources, collects the results and merges them into a single results list.

File transfer protocol (FTP)

File transfer protocol, allows transfer of files across a network from one computer to another.

Firewall

A firewall protects a network or a single computer from unauthorised Internet users. All Internet traffic is passed through the firewall, which checks each data packet against the security criteria. The firewall can block unwanted or unsafe data packets, based on settings by the network administrator. For example, a firewall can block all chat (instant messaging) software from being used across the Internet, if this is judged as unwanted. A firewall can be software, hardware or a combination of both.

Fuzzy search

A fuzzy search not only retrieves results which exactly match the query keywords, but also retrieves words with a similar spelling. For example, a fuzzy search on 'organisation' will also return 'organization', the misspelled word 'organization' and 'organised'. This results in a longer list of possibly relevant documents.

Graphical user interface (GUI)

The GUI (pronounced 'goo-ey') uses computer graphics to interact with the user. The GUI has icons, buttons, text boxes, windows etc. to visually represent the different elements of a computer that the user can interact with. The user has a mouse, which controls a pointer on the screen to select or move different objects on the screen.

The GUI is more intuitive and easier to use than a command based text interface, such as MS-DOS which was used before the introduction of the GUI.

Hypertext markup language (HTML)

HTML is the web page description language, enabling a document to be correctly displayed in a web browser. HTML uses tags in the web document to identify which lines should be bold, underlined or in a different colour. It also enables hyperlinking: the user can click on an image or word and then be taken to a different web page or image.

Information architecture

This describes the design, organisation, and navigation of information aimed at making it easier and more intuitive for a user to find and manage information. The information architecture describes the different components in the architecture, such as the user interface, taxonomy, search engine and web pages and their interaction.

For more information, see Chapter 13.

Integrated library system (ILS)

The ILS is a collection of collaborating library subsystems acting as one software application to support library processes, such as circulation, cataloguing, OPAC, acquisitions and serial control. Every subsystem uses the same underlying database with information on the library catalogue, users, vendors, etc.

Internet service provider (ISP)

This is a company that provides access to the Internet for other companies or end users. Some ISPs offer extra services like virus checking, website hosting or exclusive content (e.g. music) for members.

Intranet

Using Internet technology, an organisation can create an intranet which is only accessible to members of the organisation. The intranet is separated from the Internet by firewalls and is usually heavily protected to guard confidential information on the intranet.

Internet protocol (IP) number

This is a unique number for each computer (or other hardware) connected to the Internet. The number consists of four parts separated by dots (e.g. 214.12.12.99).

Java

This is a programming language that has been designed that it can run on many different platforms (e.g. Windows, Unix). Java is most often used to create small programs called applets that are run on a web page. As Java is platform independent, programmers only have to develop one Java applet to serve all kinds of different computer types.

JavaScript

Just like Java, JavaScript is a programming language that can be used to create scripts to add interactivity or dynamic content on a web page. JavaScript is simpler to understand than Java, but they are not related.

JPEG

The acronym for Joint Photographic Experts Group, which is the industry standard group that created it. Pronounced as 'jay-peg' it is a compression technique for images. Often also referred to as 'jpg', which is the extension used in filenames for JPEG images.

The compression used is 'lossy,' meaning that image quality is lost when the image is compressed. JPEG compressed images are usually tuned for usage on websites, as they are still detailed enough for a computer screen and small enough to transfer rather quickly. However, such a compressed image is not suited for printing.

Keywords in context (KWIC)

A technique that takes the query expression or words one searched for and displays them in the centre of the page, surrounded by accompanying text.

Legacy system

Hardware or software that has been inherited from languages, platforms, and techniques prior to 'state of the art' technology, but which the organisation can not or does not want to upgrade to the latest standard. Often the legacy system will not be compatible with the latest standard, meaning that, for example, documents and data can not be exchanged between the legacy application and the latest standard application.

Local area network (LAN)

The LAN is the network that connects computers within an office or group of buildings. The LANs allow the sharing of resources (for example, printers and shared hard disks) and the exchange of data.

The difference between the LAN and an intranet is that the LAN is the underlying infrastructure, which the intranet uses to connect users and the intranet server.

Machine-readable cataloguing record (MARC)

This is a standardised record format used by library systems for sharing and storing cataloguing information about bibliographic materials. A MARC record includes: (1) an item description, (2) main entry and added entries, (3) subject headings, and (4) the classification or call number. MARC records will often contain additional information as well, but the above is considered to be a minimum.

Metadata

Data about data, consisting of attributes (also called 'tags') that describe the data, such as the author, publication date, file size or description. The information which a library stores on an index card or in a catalogue record about a book is the metadata of the book. Metadata can be categorised into three groups: (1) *descriptive* – information describing the item, such as title, author and subject; (2) *administrative* – these items contain information about the acquisition, access control, file size etc.; and (3) *structural* – information about the structure of the data, such as the table of contents.

Online public access catalogue (OPAC)

This is the module of the library system that provides users access to the library catalogue via a GUI or web interface.

Optical character recognition (OCR)

An application that uses a bit-mapped image produced by a scanner and converts the pixels of the image into readable text by 'recognising' fonts. The OCR software has been trained to recognise different character sets and fonts, and can be further trained to improve quality.

Plug-in

A small software program that enhances the features of a larger program, such as a web browser. A plug-in can, for example, be used to offer streaming video through the web browser, without downloading a full application to the end user's computer.

Precision

The information retrieval performance measure that quantifies the fraction of retrieved documents which are known to be relevant to the end user. This measurement is often used to benchmark search engines. For example, if a query returns 25 documents and 20 of those are judged as relevant, then the search engine has a high precision. Precision and recall are the two most used measurements to test the quality of search engines and information retrieval systems in general.

Recall

Before the introduction of search engines, recall was mostly known as the definition of a request to return library material before the due date. Nowadays, recall is more used as the information retrieval performance measure that quantifies the fraction of known relevant documents which were retrieved.

In relation to precision, this is the degree to which a search engine returns all the matching documents in a collection. For example, there may be 100 matching documents, but a search engine may only find 80 of them. It would then list these 80 and have a recall of 80 per cent.

Relevancy

This is the level of how closely the search results match the search query. Search engines usually display results sorted by relevancy.

Remote access

The ability to access a computer or network from a location not directly connected to that computer or network.

Request for information (RFI)

The request that an organisation sends to vendors for information on software or hardware. It is a formal document prepared in order to request information from a vendor on products, capabilities, prices, and services. By using an RFI, an organisation can gain more information before going into a more formal negotiation.

Request for proposal (RFP)

Usually the follow-up to an RFI. A formal open-bid document that an organisation uses to request a structured response from a vendor. The template is defined by the organisation and due to its structure, different vendors can be compared on services, features, pricing, etc.

RSS

Depending on who you ask, this acronym stands for RDF Site Summary, Rich Site Summary or Really Simple Syndication. Based on XML, RSS is used to syndicate news and content of websites to end users. Instead of end users browsing a list of sites to see what's new, end users can use a so-called RSS reader application which pulls the RSS 'feeds' from relevant sites.

Server

A computer connected to a network that contains applications or data, shared by users of the network. A server can also run a specific service for the network users, such as handling e-mail. Each user connects to the mail server which acts like a post office.

Stemming

The expansion of queries to include plural forms and other word variations, by determining the grammatical root of a word. For example, when someone searches for 'computer', results returned would also include computing, computers and computation.

Storage medium

The types of media used to store computer data, such as a hard disk drive, a ZIP disk, a CD-ROM or a DAT tape.

Thin client

This is in effect a stripped down personal computer, and can be considered to be the modern version of the terminal. The thin client relies on a central server for applications and data storage, therefore not relying on applications stored locally.

Transmission control protocol/Internet protocol (TCP/IP)

The communication protocol that enables communication between all computers on the Internet. The IP component of TCP/IP enables the routing of data packets ('blocks' of data) from the local network to the enterprise network, then to regional networks, and finally to the Internet. The TCP protocol handles error detection or lost data. In such a case it asks to retransmit a data packet until the data are received complete and without errors.

Uniform resource locator (URL)

The address computers use to locate websites and web pages on the Internet, such as *www.heye.nl*.

Web browser

Often referred to as simply a browser, this is a software application that allows you to view web pages. The browser translates the web page (be it in HTML, XML, Java or another web language) to your screen. Popular browsers are Microsoft Internet Explorer, Firefox and Mozilla.

When you type an URL in the address bar of your browser, the browser does the following:

- it determines what protocol to use (usually HTTP, but could also be FTP);
- it contacts the domain name server to find the address of the server;
- it contacts the server and requests the document you pointed it to;
- it interprets the HTML page (or equivalent) and displays it on your browser.

It then awaits your input, for example clicking on a hyperlink to undertake new action.

What you see is what you get (WYSIWYG)

Pronounced 'wizzy-wig'. For word processors and desktop publishing applications this means that what you see on the screen corresponds to what you will get as printed output. In the case of web page editors like Microsoft Frontpage or Dreamweaver, it means that the file you are editing is displayed as it will appear to an end-user.

Wizard

An interactive help utility that guides the user through a potentially complex task. Examples of wizards include:

- software installation wizards which take you through all the steps of correctly installing the software;

- wizards to guide you through processes, such as a mail merge in Microsoft Word.

eXtensible markup language (XML)

Where HTML is the language used which controls how documents should be displayed, XML is more rich language. XML documents are encoded with a meaningful structure and semantics that both computers and humans can understand.

When a developer has the XML definition ('schema') for a collection of data, a script or application can be created to request, process and display data according to the schema. XML could be used, for example, to process invoices: the price in the document could be tagged ('coded') with 'price' and the invoice number with 'invoice_no'. A programmer could then write a script to calculate the total prices of this week's invoices.

Z39.50

Defined by the National Information Standards Organisation (NISO) this allows library applications to access remote library collections. To be more specific, the Z39.50 protocol defines a protocol how the query and response should be handled. In recent years, Z39.50 is being overtaken by the use of XML.

15

You can manage a project

Organisations will set up projects to make improvements in services and products. Working on a project requires different skills than being in day-to-day operations. Especially when you are requested to set up and lead a project, you will need project management skills and experience to achieve success.

Ever since I started as an information professional, I have combined jobs where providing services and managing projects were mixed. I like this kind of combination, as it gives me the best of both worlds: working with end users on a daily basis by providing them information management services and doing projects to improve products and services. All my project proposals are based on experiences I have had in my daily interaction with end users. This provides me with valuable insights to what can be improved to drive down costs and enhance value for better service to end users.

Simply stated, a project is an undertaking with a start and end time to create a unique product or service. The undertaking means that a project requires effort and resources: people, tools, money, blood, sweat and tears. A project should always have a start and end time, which makes it different from a normal daily service. It is very frustrating to be in a project that never seems to finish, or to look forward to a project that does not seem to begin. This is almost always due to bad project planning, and can seriously endanger the success of a project. Finally, the project should deliver a unique product or service – something that did not exist before the project was started.

The main steps

The main steps in a project are summarised below.

Define the project scope

This describes the boundaries of the project and clearly defines what the project will and will not deliver. For example, the goal of your project may be to implement a new intranet search engine. You define that software installation, configuration and end user testing are in the scope. However, you specifically exclude end user training as that will be part of a different project. This makes it clear to all, including your management, project members and end users what you will and will not be doing.

Write a project plan

The project plan simply defines who will be doing what and by when to achieve the goal of your project. The project plan should have dates, names and milestones to track the progress of the project when it is being executed. Where needed, dependencies between project tasks are defined.

The plan also details a cost structure for the whole project to provide management and stakeholders with insight into the costs of delivering the goal of the project.

Usually, the bigger the project is regarding time scale, costs and people involved, the more detailed the project plan will be.

Approval and resourcing

Before the project can start, it needs approval. This is usually done by the project sponsor: those who are responsible for funding and steering the project. Based on a business case (which is a document which justifies the commitment of resources to the project) and the project plan, a go or no-go decision is taken. Approval of the project also entails the commitment of the necessary resources, i.e. the budget, people and tools. As resources are always constrained, this approval is vital to achieve the success of the project.

Start the project

If you are the project manager, you will communicate the start of the project to both the project members and the stakeholders. Everyone should be clear what the project plan entails and what specific input is required from them. You will have to explain to people when they need to cooperate or when one project task depends on another.

Monitoring progress

After the project starts, it needs to be monitored according to the agreed plan. Using agreed dates and milestones, the project manager keeps their finger on the pulse of the project. Using regular project meetings, the status is discussed and eventual problems are identified including ways to solve them without endangering the project's success.

Ending the project

Wrapping up the project properly is as important as starting it. The project manager must ensure that all project goals are met and will meet with the project sponsors. The main topics of discussion will be the goals of the project and whether it was delivered on time and within budget. If there are discrepancies in the costs and delivery time, the reasons will be explained and recorded for further projects which may be similar.

Finally, the end of the project is the time when all project members and stakeholders can celebrate after all the hard work – it lifts everyone's spirit and builds commitment for further projects.

Techniques and tips

This chapter is not intended as a complete course in project management – that would require a book in itself. If you regularly work in projects or are responsible for leading projects, I recommend you follow a project management training course. This will provide you with a theoretical foundation of project management and help you build your project management skills.

Additional techniques and tips that I have learned over the years to enhance your project management skills are detailed below.

Avoid scope creep

When the project scope is agreed – stick to it. It may be tempting to include an extra task or another team, but this will not help you deliver what you agreed. It will also open the door for even more extra work, and in the end the project will either never finish or become too complex to be finished.

One of the professional project managers I once worked with had a little red, credit card sized warning sign with 'WARNING – Scope Creep!' printed on it in bold type. Whenever someone wanted to add something to the project, he would draw that card and bring the conversation back to the original scope. If the customer or manager insisted that the project should include that extra work, the project manager would refer this to the project sponsor. Ultimately, the project sponsor is responsible for agreeing what is in and out of scope, having been informed by the project manager what the extra work would entail for the deadline and resources.

Resist perfection

Avoid the temptation to do everything perfectly as this will endanger your project deadline and budget. If you think the final service or product can be even made better, define a next phase for the project. If you try and make everything perfect, it is likely your project will never end.

Positioning the project

If you are thinking about setting up a project, you must be able to sell the project to management and stakeholders. Your project should fit the strategic direction of your department or organisation to get proper support. Each project requires resources and entails a risk – so getting the proper support for your project is vital. The closer your project can be linked to key goals of higher plans, the easier it will be to get support.

If your project promises to deliver an interdepartmental document archiving standard, and one of your organisation's key objectives is to standardise and drive down costs, you can link your project to that objective. Calculate how much money and time is currently spent on document archiving, and the potential risks. Then do the same for the future scenario once your interdepartmental document archiving standard is implemented, linking this to the organisation objectives.

Get all-round buy-in

Before you start the project, identify all the teams and managers that are likely to be affected by your project. These are your stakeholders and their buy-in for the project is essential. When you are seeking the buy-in from stakeholders, make sure the right level of management approves the buy-in. Depending on how the project will utilise resources and affect stakeholders, higher levels of buy-in are needed. To avoid conflicts later on, document the buy-in of the different stakeholders by an e-mail confirmation or even written confirmation.

The most important stakeholder is the project sponsor: the manager within your organisation at a senior level who can endorse the project, ensuring the human and financial resources required are made available. The project sponsor is also ultimately responsible for requested changes to the scope or budget, in addition to the go/no-go decision to implement changes.

Document dependencies

No project is an island. Your project will depend on other activities outside your project, and the project itself will consist of interdependent tasks. If, for example, you want to open a 24/7 virtual reference service, you are dependent on actual humans being available 24/7 and IT infrastructure for the service.

In your project plan, document all dependencies inside and outside of the project. Pay particular attention to those dependencies outside of your project that are critical to your success. Make your stakeholders understand why this is critical and if you can influence that task outside of your project to your benefit. Overall, a mitigation plan for all critical dependencies should be defined: how will you influence those critical tasks? Is there a plan B?

The right stuff

When it comes to choosing the right people for the project team, strive to get the people on board who have the right mix of skills and experience. Be wary of managers volunteering some of their employees because they are available. Work with your project sponsor to get the 'best men' in your project to make it a success.

In order to get the right resources, you can try and enthuse both the employee you want on your project team and their manager. Have an informal chat or lunch with the employee and get to know what they are looking for in a new challenge. If your project has something in it for them, describe to them what the project is about and what their role could be. Focus on what they could bring into the project and most importantly, what they will gain from participating. Someone may be looking for a project to get a chance of showing their leadership skills because they would like a promotion next year. You could then offer them a leading role in a subpart of the project.

Also meet with the manager of the employee and discuss how your project would fit their agenda and goals. Describe how their employee would be of value to the project and that it would be a win-win situation for all involved.

Of course, it will depend on the culture in the organisation whether you speak to the manager or the employee first!

Honesty pays

Whether you are a project manager or a project participant, be honest about (lack of) progress and deadlines. Your input in the project does influence other project participants and the project at large, so not being totally honest endangers the overall success.

If you are a project manager, ensure all participants that you will always listen if they are honest. When a deadline cannot be met or a milestone is in danger, guarantee that you will work with your project team to help them solve it as long as they are honest. If project members do not feel comfortable reporting lack of progress, you may find out too late to solve the problem.

Project team meetings

At the start of the project the project manager defines how often and when project team meetings are held. A schedule is defined, including the meeting chairperson and team member charged with taking notes.

It may sound a bit childish, but during the first meeting state the ground rules of the meeting. For example:

- Attending the project team meeting is a priority for all. If you cannot attend, notify the chairperson in advance and let them know what your reported progress and issues are.

- If a team member knows in advance they will be absent and have a role in the meeting (e.g. chairperson, taking notes or presenting), they will arrange for a substitute.

- Cell phones, pagers, Blackberries and the like are turned off for the duration of the meeting.

- Too detailed or lengthy discussions are either taken offline or scheduled for a separate meeting with the team members involved.

- Everyone listens to one another.

- The chairperson is the time keeper and has the right to intervene when items take too long or are not relevant for the meeting.

- Minutes will be distributed within 24 hours of the meeting.

- The agenda of the next meeting is distributed to all members x days before the meeting is held.

Team meetings have different purposes, including team building, problem recognition, planning and decision making.

Having an agenda is key to a good meeting. The agenda tells project members up front what will be discussed and when. Project members can submit items for the meeting agenda until a certain time before the meeting, but a general template for the agenda is defined in the first meeting.

Following the meeting, the meeting minutes are a record of what of was discussed and decided. If there is confusion later on, the meeting minutes will provide clarity to settle the issue.

The meeting minutes should also contain a list of action items, as detailed below.

Assign action items

During project meetings, keep a running list of action items that have come up during the discussions. Before you conclude the meeting, run through the list of items and assign each action to a person with a deadline. Do not assign an action to a team, but to a person – if you assign it to a team, everyone in that team will think that the other is responsible.

During the next project meeting, tick off the actions items from the last meeting. I would recommend you contact all project members with action items halfway between two meetings, to make sure they will be able to act upon all action items.

Delegate

If you are the project manager, you will have to delegate certain tasks to project team members in order to free up your time to focus on project management. It also means that you can assign certain responsibilities to team members who are better qualified to do a certain task, such as budget maintenance or project public relations.

Keep in mind that even though you assign a certain task to a team member, i.e. give them the authority to take certain decisions, you will still be responsible for the outcome of that task.

Risk management

When the project starts, a risk analysis should be executed. Brainstorm with the project team members what risks could occur, under which circumstances and their impact on the project. Then rank all the risks to determine which risks should be avoided or mitigated and how. If a similar project has been executed before, the post mortem review of that project will have key learnings regarding project risks for your project.

Communication is key

Be sure to include communication activities as important tasks in your project plan, as your stakeholders should be updated regularly about the project. Define who should be targeted with different communication media, for example, a regular face-to-face meeting with top management, a weekly newsletter for the intended end users and a website with daily updates for the departments involved in delivering the project.

By means of communication you keep everybody who is relevant to the project involved and updated. Communication should be open and clear about the progress and changes to the plan, if they occur.

Plan for quality check and rework

If your project concerns building a product, plan enough time for quality checking and reworking. If you do not plan for quality check, you may be surprised at the end that your new content management system or your automated book scanning appliance do not work properly. Check regularly for the required quality and schedule rework time after every quality check. If no time for rework is planned, your project schedule will slip behind schedule. However, if you schedule for rework but do not need it, you will be ahead of schedule, which you will certainly need for unplanned events.

Find a champion

Where the project sponsor decides on the project from a high level, a project sponsor helps to build support for the project on a political level and act as a spokesperson. The ideal project sponsor has an interest in the project outcomes, has influence and can convince others about the necessity of the project. They are not be involved in the project, but advise on communication issues, and help to achieve proper buy-in or support when needed.

When I was leading a project on an organisation-wide knowledge database, I found a senior vice president in human resources as a project champion. He was fierce believer in connecting all staff in order to share experience and knowledge, so he often spoke enthusiastically about the project during management meetings. When the project launched, he wrote a glowing recommendation letter to all participating employees, encouraging them to participate. This was a big help in getting a firm start in the development of the knowledge database.

Balancing day-to-day work and project work

If you have to combine a day job and project work, you will have to be strict on what you can and cannot do. The combination of a day job and projects could mean that the projects get in the way of the day job and vice versa. When you take on project work, agree with management how your time is spent and where priorities lie. To the extent possible, define how much time the project work will take and block that in your calendar.

I have always combined a day job with project work and block the hours per day that I will be working on projects. This way I know where the split between my activities is and how to keep them separate. It also avoids bad planning where the project or the day job takes over the majority of the work hours of the other.

If possible, find backup resources for critical times when you are stuck with a crisis in your day job or project. Another colleague might be able to step in temporarily for your day job when your project work needs your complete attention.

Decision making

During the project many decisions will have to be taken. The smaller decisions will be taken by the project member who is responsible without involving others. When a decision is more complex, and others inside or outside the project need to be involved, it may get problematic if it is not clear within the project team how decisions are taken.

Essentially, there are three different models of decision making:

- *Directive*: In this model, the project manager makes all the complex decisions. The advantage is that it is very clear who will take the decision, and decision making can be very fast. The drawback is that the project manager may not be the right person to take a decision, as they do not have all the information or experience. In addition, the project team members will feel left out of the decision-making process, especially if they do not agree with the decision being taken by the project manager. This model can best be used when there is no time or opportunity to consult all necessary team members, but a decision needs to be made or otherwise the future of the project is immediately at stake.

- *Participative*: Everyone in the team has the same level of decision making and all are allowed to contribute. Highly democratic, and all will feel involved in the decision being taken – and the outcome. Even when the decision is not what everyone would do, each team member has had a chance to contribute and they will feel at least consulted. However, taking decisions this way takes more time and can lead to compromises. The project manager should decide when this decision-making model is best used – the fundamental decisions in the project are most often where full team commitment is required.

■ *Consultative*: Between directive and participative decision making is the consultative model. The project manager still takes the decision, but this is only done after consulting the required team members. Instead of having to wait until all team members are available to deliver their input and come to a decision, the project manager collects the required input and bases their decision on that. This model is the one most recommended for the majority of the decisions to be taken in the project, as this balances correctly between the commitment required and the necessary time spent by project members contributing to the decision.

Post mortem review

When the project has ended, schedule one final meeting with stakeholder representatives, project sponsor and the project team members for the so-called post mortem review. The project is over, but now is the time to review it and learn from what went well and what went wrong. Check what the project delivered against the project plan and whether it is delivered on time and within budget.

The stakeholders and project sponsor now have the chance to look back on what they thought the project would establish and whether that was achieved. Do not forget to analyse the project way of working: was there tension in the project? How was that handled? What would project members have done differently in hindsight?

Document the post mortem review and distribute the learnings among those who were involved and those outside the project who are interested. Others will be able to leverage from what your project has achieved and will also learn from your mistakes.

Gannt chart

A Gannt chart is one of the most useful project management tools, as it helps to keep track of progress for project activities. Due to its graphical nature, the Gannt chart allows non-project managers to quickly understand the project flow and start of discussions on the project timeline and activities. Using this type of chart, it is easy to see how the project is planned and when activities overlap or are dependent on one another.

When you have defined all the activities in your project, use a spreadsheet to set up a Gannt chart. On the horizontal axis of the Gannt chart you put the timeline of the project, be it in days, weeks or months. This depends on the complexity and length of the project. On the vertical axis of the chart you put all the activities in the order they have to be executed. Use colours to group certain activities and list milestones of the project in the chart.

Then draw lines for each activity for the scheduled length of that activity. The start point is in the column where the activity begins and the end of the line is the column when the activity should end.

By looking at the current date on the Gannt chart, the project manager and project members can see what activities should be finished by now, which are underway and which lie ahead. If hiccups occur during the project, causing disruption to the planning, the Gannt chart can be used to redraw the project planning, for example, by extending the time for certain activities or rescheduling activities for a future date.

16

You know how to effectively market yourself

Information professionals usually don't consider marketing themselves as a big issue. After all, we are the key to all the information, we are service and customer oriented, we know our business – so customers will just come to us, right?

Unfortunately, even though all of the above is true, we need to market ourselves. Not just to be known, but also to let our customers know who we are and what we can do to help them.

Our customers have many choices in getting information, and information professionals are not always the first they think of. As information professionals, we often see the Internet as our biggest competitor. We should learn to see that the Internet can only prove our value even more – but our most fearsome enemy is not being used. Amid the information explosion, our customers think that they do not need our services, our catalogues or our database expertise.

We are in the complex business of professional services, which are, in essence, intangible: you cannot touch them as they are mostly about advice, ideas and recommendations. Unlike products, professional services cannot be tried or sampled before they are acquired. Unlike marketing a product, this makes marketing professional services more challenging and a necessity.

In this chapter I will share my experiences with marketing myself successfully as information professional inside and outside my organisation.[1]

The bottom line

In his book *The Brand Gap*, Mart Neumeier addresses three questions on building a brand which are also key to marketing yourself:

1. Who are you?
2. What do you do?
3. Why does it matter?

The first question is the easiest one, but the second and third are harder to answer. 'What do you do?' should address the unique selling points of your services in the eye of the customer. If you are a literature searcher, that is what you do – but what does that mean for the customer? Basically what you do is provide customers a good overview of published and grey literature on a certain topic, focused on their particular problem to help them solve a problem or make a decision.

This then ties in to the third question, which should be the most compelling to the customer: why does it matter to *me* what you do? This last answer should directly link your services to the benefit that the client is after.

Customer focus

Keep in mind when you are marketing your services that you have to focus on the benefits the customer wants as a result of your services. In this case, if you provide a literature search service, the benefit for the customer is that they get a good overview of existing literature and avoid re-inventing the wheel. This translates then into saving money for the customer.

If you have a list of your services, describe from the viewpoint of the customer and link them to a direct and recognisable benefit for them. Make clear how your services make a valuable contribution to that benefit, as that is what will get the customer's attention.

Promote your services portfolio

If you have defined your services portfolio following the advice above, make sure your portfolio is ready at hand for your customers when they need it. Nowadays it is essential to put your services portfolio online, but do not forget to create print versions. These can be handed out when meeting customers, giving them something to read immediately. Providing them with a link requires another action on their end, namely going online, which will reduce the chances of them seeing your portfolio.

As an example, I worked as an information specialist in a large, multinational company, so a lot of my clients were not in the same building, the same continent or time zone. To be noticed, I had set up a short, informative web page about my services within the library group on the company intranet. This made it very easy for my current and potential customers to find my list of services and samples.

Every week I devote time to browsing and reading internal discussion forums, and trying to participate in discussion by providing references, pointing to online and offline sources or offering to set up a literature search for them. Every time, at the bottom of my reply is a pointer to my services website.

Find champions

In order to attract new business, a champion can be very useful. A champion is a person within your target audience who knows your qualities and services, and is willing to carry your story forward to others. The champion does not have to be a customer themselves, but can connect you to potential new customers. As the champion is seen as a trustworthy person by your target audience, it is a very good introduction for you to others.

In order to find a champion, look for senior management or key roles in the customer's organisation. The champion has a wide network within the organisation and is recognised as a leading figure, which makes them trusted by customers. They can advise you on the proper way of finding new customers, understanding the organisation and generally championing your services.

When I worked for a consultancy firm as an information specialist, one of the senior managers was my champion. After I had performed several last-minute heroics for him on finding obscure information, he introduced me to his whole team. In an e-mail he described how I had saved his day several times and had shown to be a human search engine, urging others to use my services instead of looking for information themselves. Frequently I would catch up with him, getting inside information on the information needs of the consultancy group and being introduced to potential new customers via him.

Stay in touch

Ask someone how they are doing, and very often you will get the answer: busy. Our lives seem run at a higher speed than those of our parents and grandparents, which is why we often seem to get caught in a whirlwind. At work, this is no different, and there seems to be less time to do more every year.

As a service professional, make it a habit to stay in touch with your colleagues, your customers, your potential customers and your champions. Do this on a regular basis, so that they do not forget about you. Spending time with colleagues or customers is an investment in your future, as you will learn more about them and very often be remembered of when your services are required.

Very often, people will be reminded of what they wanted to ask you: a research request, a question about that new database system or advice on finding competitor information.

If your customers or champions are very busy and it is hard for you to simply 'drop by', you can meet them over a cup of coffee or perhaps during lunch. We all have to eat, don't we? During those short meetings, get to know more about what's keeping them busy and see how you could help them. Build a network of people, so you have feelers out in your organisation to keep you up to date and in the loop. You will be amazed how much more work will be referred to you and how easier it gets to build business cases.

Participate in clients' meetings

A more regular way to stay up to date with your customers is to participate in their team meetings. Try to find out what team is meeting when, and whether you can be present. Explain that this is a very efficient way for you to get informed on what is going on, so you can proactively provide services. During those meetings you could supply information on agenda topics or suggest training for relevant online and offline sources.

When possible, I scan and browse relevant industry journals related to my clients' business. This way I pick up trends, pointers to relevant publications and I learn their jargon. By being able to speak my clients' language, or at least show that I am interested in their world I am taken seriously.

Publish about your professional interests

To be noticed outside my organisation, I have created a website (*www.dennie.heye.nl*) which links to my presentations and articles. This has proven to be very useful when I am asked to present at a conference or write an article – by providing one link, I share my portfolio of writing.

Nowadays, within a few minutes you can publish a website yourself by writing a web log, or 'blog' as they are commonly known.

A web log is mostly a personal website in a dated log format on a particular topic or interest, updated on a very frequent basis. Web logs often point to items on other websites and comment on them, which makes them great places to visit for staying up to date while just visiting a small number of web logs. Often, blogs have a feature where readers can comment on the posting, making this more interactive than a normal website.

Chapter 17 lists pointers to relevant blogs and directories of blogs that might be of interest to you.

You can set up a blog about your professional interests, sharing links to relevant stories with your comments and views, or post articles on your developments. Once again, think from a reader's perspective: what's in it for them? What will readers gain from your blog: useful tips and tricks for search engines, insights into taxonomies or an interesting journal about the life of a cataloguer? Make sure you have the time and creativity to keep updating your blog and promote it.

Clear message

During all my communications, be it a PowerPoint presentation, a website or a face-to-face meeting with a new clients, I always try to be clear on the services I provide. I emphasise my key advantages as a literature searcher: I have access to a variety of quality information; a wide network; professional knowledge of interviewing, searching and dissemination; and last but not least I can provide better information faster and cheaper. Honesty is also something I emphasise – I do not promise what I cannot deliver, even though there sometimes is pressure to do so. On an annual basis, via an anonymous feedback form I ask my clients to provide comments on my services, providing me with new ideas for improvement. To get more feedback on my professional performance, I ask trusted colleagues (from different departments) to tell me honestly what they think of my services or approach.

Networking

Both inside and outside my organisation I consider networking to be essential to my job. I've joined several informal groups within my organisation (e.g. a network of young professionals, the literature researchers' group) and attend monthly meetings of different teams. This brings me into contact with a wide variety of colleagues, and I often get referrals via someone I've met during my networking.

When someone has met you, even though it may have been only briefly during an event where you explained what you do, it is far more likely that they will refer a colleague to you.

Outside my organisation, I am member of a professional library organisation and participate in the alumni committee of the college where I received my library sciences degree. Via these networks I learn about best practices on marketing myself as an information professional and am always just a phone call away from a peer to discuss.

Do read the specific chapter on networking in this book, as it contains many more tips and strategies.

A final tip on marketing yourself as information professional is to learn from others. Look around in your organisation, in your peer group or your neighbourhood for people who you consider to be good at marketing themselves. If possible, try and meet them to ask them about their ideas and experiences.

Note

1. This chapter is a rewritten and expanded version of an article that originally appeared in the September 2004 issue of the Info Career Trends newsletter (*http://www.lisjobs.com/newsletter*).

You are always up to date

As an information professional it is essential to stay up to date on the industry you are working in, your organisation and your profession. In these days of information floods and a jungle of websites, however, finding the right information and keeping up to date with it is not so easy. This chapter describes tools and techniques to help you with this.

Tools and techniques

I have used a variety of tools and techniques to keep abreast of developments in my field, so I can recommend following to keep you up to date.

E-mail

Before the wonder of RSS, which delivered headlines automatically to your RSS reader, there has always been e-mail. As not all websites offer RSS feeds, or if you prefer e-mail, you will be pleased to find that many websites offer an e-mail service to deliver new items or headlines to you. There is also the ancient Internet technology of the mailing list, which is still extremely powerful.

This is a really quick way to stay up to date, as you don't have to surf through several websites to see what's new, but get the new items delivered to you. I use a variety of e-mail news services and mailing lists, which I synchronise to my PDA. Then I catch up on what is new when I am waiting for a meeting to start, during my daily commute or during a coffee break.

For a good start to find a mailing list on your topic, surf to *http://www.topica.com*, while for newsgroups there's the vast collection at *http://groups.google.com*. One great example of a mailing list for information professionals is Free Pint (*http://www.freepint.com*). This high-quality newsletter brings about 44,000 information professionals around the globe together in a virtual way. Each issue brings articles on a specific topic with links to the best websites, written by an expert information professional. Another not to be missed mailing list is SearchDay, a daily newsletter from SearchEngineWatch with the latest on Web searching tools, techniques and tips (*http://searchenginewatch.com/*).

Customised profiles and search alerts

You can subscribe to online services like Dialog, Lexis-Nexis or Factiva which have really powerful profiling features and can deliver information matching your profile by e-mail. For example, I've set up profiles which track my company's competitors. The minute they announce a new service or issue a press release relating to one of the topics I'm interested in, I get an e-mail with a link to the full text article.

Website changes trackers like WatchThatPage (*http://www.watchthatpage.com/*) are another helpful tool using e-mail. Say, you've found a couple of great websites with subjects you want to stay on top of, but they do not offer a RSS feed or an e-mail service. You can now point WatchThatPage to track updates to complete websites or a single page and receive e-mail alerts about the changes. I use this to track our competitors'websites and learn about their new services and products.

Related to this are search engine alert services like Google Alerts (*www.google.com/alerts*). You specify a search string, and your friends at Google send you an e-mail when a new hit matching your search string has been found in news headlines, the Web or in UseNet discussion groups. This frees you from doing regular searches with search engines.

Blogs and RSS

To stay on top of breaking news, I was delighted to find the wonderful invention of the web log (or blog) a few years ago. A web log is a website, mostly in a dated log format on a particular topic or interest, updated on a very frequent basis.

Blogs often point to items on other websites and comment on them, which makes them great places to visit for staying up to date while just visiting a small number of web logs. Almost all blogs offer a so-called RSS feed, which is a technology that can deliver the blog updated headlines to your RSS reader. The RSS reader can be an application on the Web or installed on your computer, that pulls the requested RSS feeds from the blogs or websites you have identified. Instead of browsing all the websites you are interested in, one scan through your RSS reader shows you all that is new.

On library topics, Librarian.net (*http://www.librarian .net/*) and Library Crunch (*http://www.librarycrunch.com/*)

are two of my favourite library web logs. They bring news and comments on relevant library issues. In addition, I'd certainly recommend you take a look at my favourite web log on information searching: The ResourceShelf (*http://www.resourceshelf.com/*). Gary Price and his team post new and interesting websites for researchers every day, with comments. This blog may point you to obscure, but highly recommended websites and online resources that will make your research a lot easier.

For a directory of web logs, sorted by topic, go to the Open Directory project at *http://dmoz.org/Computers/ Internet/On_the_Web/Web_Logs/*. Specifically for library and information science related web logs, there is an excellent directory at LibDex (*http://www.libdex.com/ weblogs.html*)

And lastly, I've installed the RSS news ticker on my desktop (*http://www.rssnewsticker.com/*) which brings me real-time news on my particular interests even when I am not watching my RSS reader. There are many, many topics to choose from, or you can use keyword search to create your own news ticker. When I see an interesting story, I immediately post a link on our intranet or send the link to someone who may be interested in it.

Real people

Not a technology, but a truly wonderful source of staying up to date is talking to real people. Your colleagues, your manager, industry or topical experts and your peers are great sources for news and insights. In this age of the Web and chatting, a regular face-to-face discussion is still highly valuable. It not only brings you up to date on what is going on, it also helps you to develop your network!

Trade and professional magazines

Paper has been declared dead several times in recent years, but for trade and professional magazines paper is still the main medium. It is easy to read in bed, in the bath or on the train. When the article is longer than one page, it is particularly convenient to read it on paper. For information professionals, there is a variety of magazines that deliver relevant news and insightful articles.

If you join a professional association like the Special Libraries Association (SLA) or the International Federation of Library Associations and Institutions (IFLA), you will automatically be subscribed to their journal. There are many other professional magazines, each with different scope and audience.

Online journals

Almost all journals in the field of information professionals now have an electronic counterpart, and a growing number exists only online. For almost every area in the field of information and library science there is a dedicated journal or e-zine (electronic magazine). The wonderful staff of LibDex (the library index) maintain a growing list of links to library and information science online journals at *http://www.libdex.com/journals.html*.

Podcasts

Like blogs, podcasting uses RSS to deliver content to an end user. Unlike blogs, podcasts consist of audio files that can be played on your computer, iPod or other MP3 players. The podcast author publishes a new audio file to a server, which adds it as an attachment to a RSS feed. A program like iTunes will scan the RSS feeds of podcasts you are interested in and download the audio files. You can then either play the podcast on your computer or carry it with you on your MP3 player. I listen to a variety of podcasts while commuting or when I am working out in the gym.

If you are interested in Internet searching, the Daily Searchcast by Danny Sullivan is one for you (*blog .searchenginewatch.com/blog/podcast.html*). In a 10–15 minute recap, you will be updated of the latest news on the major search engine news. If you are interested in what will be the future of digital libraries, the semantic web and other relevant topics, check out 'Talking with Talis' at *http://talk.talis.com/*.

Since the initial start in 2004, many podcasts are now launched every day. To find relevant podcasts for you, start at a podcast directory like Podcast.net (*www.podcast.net*), Yahoo! Podcasts (*podcasts.yahoo.com*) or browse the podcast section of iTunes.

By using these tools I am able to support my colleagues with 'customised' real-time news, which can make a big difference. For example, a year ago my company was in fierce competition with two other companies for a major project. On the day that all the participating parties were to present their proposal for this project, I got an important search alert. This search alert told me that the client we were bidding for had just hired a new CFO, who used to be a colleague of our marketing manager. So at the last minute, our marketing manager took over the presentation from the sales manager ... and yes, we closed the deal.

Conclusion

It should be clear that the twenty-first century is the most exciting time to be an information professional. Not only can we benefit from the accelerating speed of technology and innovation, but we have a unique opportunity to be recognised as true professionals.

We must, therefore, reinvent ourselves and be equipped with a broad range of skills to tackle all the present and future challenges in our jobs.

If you have read the whole book, I would invite you to compare the level of your skills before you started reading this book and now. By applying the tips and guidance in this book, you should now have a broad understanding on the skill set you can apply in your daily job and future career.

I would like to warn you that you can read books, attend training classes and follow all the expert guidance – but in the end, the level of your success is up to you. In addition to all the aspects previously discussed, it takes determination, perseverance and a good dose of enthusiasm to be a successful twenty-first century information professional.

To sum up what you should do now you have finished this book:

■ keep learning – sign up for formal education and get relevant training by attending conferences, seminars and workshops;

- gain experience in an increasing level to allow you to reach new heights in your performance;

- if you have not already done so, get certified as an information professional – this will develop your resumé and provide you with a firm, professional foundation;

- join a professional or networking organisation to increase your learning opportunities and chances to network;

- be positive in times of change – look for the bright side and how you can learn from difficult times;

- last, but not least, you now know that we live in dynamic times as information professionals: *continuously adapt, evolve and learn to be a successful information professional.*

Bibliography

Chakrabarti, S. (2002) *Mining the Web: Discovering Knowledge from Hypertext Data.* Morgan-Kaufmann Publishers: San Francisco, CA.

Kaplan, R. and Norton. D. (1992) 'The Balanced Scorecard – measures that drive performance'. *Harvard Business Review* (Jan–Feb), pp. 71–9.

Kelley, T. and Littman J. (2001) *The Art of Innovation: Lessons in Creativity from IDEO, America's Leading Design Firm.* Doubleday Publishing: New York.

Leeds, D. (2003) *PowerSpeak: Engage, Inspire, and Stimulate Your Audience.* Career Press: New Jersey.

Mundt, S. (2003) 'Benchmarking user satisfaction in academic libraries – a case study' *Library and Information Research* 27(87): 38–46.

Neumeier M. (2005) *The Brand Gap* (2nd edn). New Riders Press: Indianapolis.

Pruitt, D. G. and Rubin, J. Z. (1986) *Social Conflict: Escalation, Stalemate and Settlement.* Random House: New York.

Rosenfeld, L. and Morville, P. (2002) *Information Architecture for the World Wide Web: Designing Large-Scale Web Sites.* O'Reilly Media: Sebastopol, CA.

Saracevic, T. and Kantor, P. B. (1997) 'Studying the value of library and information services. Part II: Methodology and taxonomy' *Journal of the American Society for Information Science*: 48(6): 543–63.

Siess, J. (2002) *Time Management, Planning and Prioritization for Librarians*. Scarecrow Press: Cleveland, OH.

Siess, J. (2003) *The Visible Librarian: Asserting Your Value with Marketing and Advocacy*. ALA Editions: Cleveland, OH.

Steckel, M. (2002) 'Ranganathan for IAs: An introduction to the thought of S.R. Ranganathan for information architects'. Boxes and Arrows', Available at: *http://www .boxesandarrows.com/view/ranganathan_for_ias* (Last accessed: 2 January 2006).

Tuckerman, B. W. (1965) 'Developmental sequence in small groups'. *Psychological Bulletin*.

Wurman, R. S. (1996) *Information Architects*. Graphis Press: Zurich.

UC Berkeley School of Information Management and Systems (2003) 'How much information is there?'. Available at: *http://www.sims.berkeley.edu/research/ projects/how-much-info-2003/execsum.htm* (Last accessed: 2 January 2006).

Index

Printed in the United Kingdom
by Lightning Source UK Ltd.
108934UKS00002B/97-147